LOVE ME RIGHT or NOT AT ALL

A Quick Guide to Loving Yourself + Others the Healthy Way

Joseph D. Snider

Love Me Right or Not At All

This book is dedicated to God and my Lord and Savior Jesus Christ! Without Your still small voice speaking to me, I wouldn't have written the words that are found on these pages.

This book is also dedicated to my wife and children for loving me through this process! It isn't an easy thing to love someone who is going through a major transformation. They weathered this storm with me. They had to love me through all my incarnations. Thank You!

I also want to say thanks to my friends Patrice, Kevin, Ashley, and Akira, you guys believed in this book before it was even written on paper. Your constant encouragement pushed me to get it done! For your encouragement I am forever grateful!

Love Me Right or Not At All

To my sisters, Stephanie and Kate, thank you for being my friends and always giving me the truth that I need to hear. That truth was some of the inspiration for this book!

Just In Case: Let me remind you who you are.....

FOREWORD BY PATRICE REYNOLDS PATE

I don't know... As I sat in silence thinking of reasons why I couldn't free my mind of this thing, I kept coming to the same conclusion; "It's you, something's just not right with you and the way you're handling this. You're not who you think you are or who you believe yourself to be. If you were, things would be different." I tossed and turned for nights on end, this thing weighing heavily on my mind. Then God unveiled truth; "You don't believe Me. It is a war of the mind. You have reached a place of 'self-control'. You are attempting to control 'self'. You MUST believe who I say you are in Me not in you. Why are you not sure? Why do you doubt who and where you are, in Me? Why do you think so lowly of Me? You are a reflection of Me. You don't believe Me when I tell you who you are." This

Love Me Right or Not At All

distraction is SELF driven and has caused a diversion; and while you're focusing on "you" a takeover, robbery, and invasion of the mind is in progress.

You were in the mind of God before man was ever created. You were all planned out and destined to be created. You were always apart and always had a part to play in His master plan. All His thoughts toward you are good and never evil. When God made you He equipped you with everything you would need to carry out your part in His plan—you already have it. He already knows you can do what he has set forth for you to do. He has loved you and has created no one like you. You are an originator and a creator just like Him. No one can take what He has given you ... ever. Being locked up, stuck, held back, forgotten about, beaten down, in a bad marriage or left alone can't even cancel what He planned for you. He created you unbreakable in what He has created you to complete. He created you wonderfully and fearfully being careful not to make a mistake. Because of Christ you are perfect in his sight. You are made RIGHT.

I wish you believed that you were elected for why you are here. You are royalty in eternity. You are not here because two teenagers whose hormones were raging out of control decided to have sex and "oops" there came you. You HAD to be brought forth. You were arriving ANYWAY through teenage sex, pre-marital sex, disturbing sex, illegal sex, rape or any other sexual situation, right or wrong. It was used as your entrance to Earth in your Earth suit. You have a true purpose on Earth and you were planned ... "Planned". Choose to do your part in His master plan, do what you were created to do and do what you were made to do. Do what only you can do.

Your Dharma

Anyone who has ever felt not good enough. A feeling of something being wrong with you. The feeling that you are missing out. The feeling of being looked over, passed by and

Love Me Right or Not At All

cast aside. "What's wrong with me?" you keep asking. If you have to remind yourself who you are constantly, this book, *Love Me Right or Not At All*, by Joseph Snider is for you. Knowing who you are will begin to bring forth healing in depression, gets rid of the "less than" feeling, helps you get through bouts of loneliness and helps get you over heartbreaks and relational disappointments quick! If you only knew that the journey you go through was NEVER about YOU personally. Every hurt and devastation you went through was not an attack on YOU personally but an attack on the earth. It's not about you. It's about destroying the equipment in you that is needed for a dying world. It's about getting you to give up and murder the very reason why you were created. There, I highlighted it for you. Many will choose another path, but what will you do? Many will reject and despise you; many will forget about you; many will try to destroy you. Many will mistreat you; many will not understand you and many will not see you. Some will hurt you by mistake or on purpose. If you could only remember who you are. If you could only wear it on your forehead, constantly hear it shouting in your ears, constantly sing it out of your mouth, and always see it in the mirror. If you could only walk as who you really are and not who you pretend to be. If you could only believe Him. Everyone has been hurt; through hurt you remain who you are. You are an upright spirit-being in a body with a soul that belongs to no one but the Creator.

It is completely impossible for you to carry out your purpose if the one that created you had not planned on you. ~ Patrice Reynolds Pate

CONTENTS

Foreword By Patrice Reynolds Pate	iv
Where Do I Start?	xi
It Is Time to Start!	1
Starting Point 1: Get over Yourself	9
Take off the Mask	9
Starting Point 1: Get over Yourself	15
Let Go Of The Past You	15
Starting Point 1: Get Over Yourself	23
Give of Yourself and Not Give To Yourself in Relationships	23
Starting Point 1: Get Over Yourself	31
Embrace the New You	31
Starting Point 2: Love Yourself Now	37
Why Love Myself after You Told Me to Get over Myself?	37
Starting Point 2: Love Yourself Now	54
Look Forward and Only Look Back to Avoid Repeating the Past	54
Starting Point 2: Love Yourself Now!	59
Remove past People from Your Present Life	59
Starting Point 2: Love Yourself Now	64
Romance Yourself	64

Starting Point 3: Give Love to the Right People	69
Identify Who Belongs in Your Life	69
Starting Point 3: Give Love to the Right People	85
Identify Who Doesn't Belong and Ask Them to Leave	85
Starting Point 3: Give Love to the Right People	90
You Will Need to Rinse and Repeat	90
Starting Point 3: Give Love to the Right People	95
Manage Love the Right Way with the Right People	95
Starting Point 4: Love with Balance	107
Keep Your Word and Be Honest	107
Starting Point 4: Love with Balance	114
Have Realistic Expectations for Them and You	114
Starting Point 4: Love with Balance	130
Admit When You're Wrong and Forgive Others	130
Starting Point 4: Love with Balance	138
Be Loyal, Show Affection, and Give Space When Needed	138
Starting Point 4: Love with Balance	155
Be in Charge of Your Own Happiness	155
Starting Point 5: Enjoy the Love You're In	167
The Here and Now Love	167
Evaluate It All	171

WHERE DO I START?

Have you ever wondered why it feels like you do nothing but fail at relationships? Do you ever think, *Why does everyone mess over me?* I have asked both of these questions before, during, and after every failed relationship. It didn't matter whether it was a friendship or an intimate relationship; it started with one of the questions above and ended with one of them too. Most of us want to be successful in our relationships; we want our marriages to be awesome, we want our friendships to last forever, we want each and every sexual encounter to be out of this world, but most of all we want people to love us. We want people to love us and for it to be right, for it to feel right, and for everything to be right in our world.

The question that continues to exist is how? How in the hell do we make things right? I have told them how I needed to be loved and they still don't get it. I've shown them how I would give them the world and they won't accept it. We have gone to counseling, prayed at the altar at church, and spent all of our money on a relationship psychic; we've read all the books, but we still don't have the right kind of relationships. So what can I write that will make things right for you and your relationships? I asked myself the same question when I decided to write this book. As you're reading this I want you to understand that no one can make relationships work for you. That is not what I'm going to promise you in this book, but I hope this book can be a guide. I want this book to be a guide to help everyone discover how to do relationships in a better way. I want better and I am hoping that, after reading this book, we get better. I don't have a cure-all, a magic lamp, or a cool mantra; but I do have a fresh perspective, and a new way to view how to navigate relationships. This book is a conversation between us. It is an intimate look at how we view ourselves and how we love ourselves. This is a conversation that I want you to listen to, learn from, and take what is said and apply it to what works for you. This book can be a guide, but it will be up to you how you

Love Me Right or Not At All will use it and implement it to have successful relationships. The race to having healthy relationships starts with how well you love yourself! That race starts right now!

IT IS TIME TO START!

Starting out on a new journey is often the most difficult part of the trip because we are dealing with many complex thoughts and feelings. We battle with doubt, fear, and trying to figure out if things will make sense at all. We question our self-confidence, our self-worth, and even if the trip will even be worth it in the end. This inner turmoil causes most people to eventually give up on the journey altogether and forfeit the chance to ever see if they could have been successful. This is true in pursuing relationships, whether platonic ones or intimate relationships, and we miss out on what could be the most amazing relationships we've ever had or the relationships that may not have been successful but were necessary in helping us learn and grow. I do understand the risk of getting into relationships and the pain that is often associated with a break up or failure, but if we never tried some of us would have never discovered that special person, our best friend, or even the significant other that, in a sense, completes us.

For this reason I decided to write this book. I wanted to give us all a chance to discover what it means to truly be loved and to get fulfillment out of the relationships that we are active participants in. I want us all to have a chance to be loved the right way and no longer have our time wasted or waste someone else's time because we refused to learn how to love them. What is more important than loving them is that most of us don't even know how to love ourselves the right way and we enter into relationships lost within our own selves. So I want to help guide us down the "rabbit hole" of where should "I" start; to introduce to you the *Five Starting Points* on how to love yourself the right way and loving others the right way as well. The Five Starting points are:

1. Get Over Yourself
2. Love Yourself Now
3. Give Love to the Right People
4. Love with Balance
5. Enjoy the Love You're In

Hopefully, as you read and dive into these chapters you will unearth what possibly has been missing in your relationships. I have identified them as starting points to help us answer the question "Where do I start?" but also to help us understand that relationships aren't linear or straightforward as we often believe or "expect" them to be; relationships can often be cyclical, or free flowing like the wind, or even more fluid and ever-changing like water. This is why we may often find ourselves evaluating or questioning our relationships, disappointed because things aren't going in a straight line or as expected, and we are constantly riddled with questions of doubt; asking what did I do wrong, why don't they love me, why do I care so much; asking will I ever find love, will I ever be appreciated, and where should I start?

That is why we have the Five Starting Points, not only to address the several questions that we have when starting a relationship or evaluating relationships we are already in, but also to help us gain a better understanding of the perspective that

Love Me Right or Not At All

the flow of relationships isn't rigid and stagnant, but constantly changing just like the individuals who engage in relationships with one another. You can start from the first starting point and move forward or you can start from the fifth starting point and move backwards. Wherever you start I just want you to be confident in starting, to truly find what could be missing by not relating to others in such a powerful, yet free and burden light way. Our relationships should not weigh us down, they should be enjoyable. We shouldn't be plagued with rigid and unreasonable expectations in our relationships, but instead communicate to those we are in relationship with our wants, needs, and desires; our friends and significant others should feel comfortable communicating to us their wants, needs, and desires. I want us to come to the realization that it is OK to restart, refresh, or renew our relationships and to do this without the fear of looking or feeling like a failure. Pressing the reset button in our relationships doesn't automatically qualify us as failures, but brings us to the important and often missed moment in our relationships: Evaluation. The Five Starting Points help us to evaluate our relationships and help us to identify what we may need to add or subtract in our intimate encounters with ourselves and with others.

Get Over Yourself and *Give Love to the Right People* are starting points one and three respectively and help us to identify who to start with. These starting points help us to evaluate who we are and who we are giving ourselves to. It is so difficult to be an effective and active participant in a relationship if you don't know yourself and you have no clue who you are in a relationship with. Not only do they help us evaluate the "who" in the relationship, but the how to do it as well. I can be honest with you now; the chapters on *Get Over Yourself* are going to be the most difficult to explore. For me this starting point was not only the most difficult to discover or even apply, but it was also the most difficult for me to write as well. I will get more into it in the next few chapters, but I wanted to give you a fair warning that, while this starting point will help you, it is going to burst

Love Me Right or Not At All

some fixed beliefs that we have held about ourselves and others; the very same beliefs that have hindered the relationships we are engaged in. *Give Love to the Right People* will hopefully not only change the way you think, look, and feel about the people you are in relationship with, but help you make better decisions about the people you choose to love. These two starting points, however, are anchored powerfully by the next two starting points.

Love Yourself Now and *Enjoy the Love You're In* are starting points two and five respectively and they help us to focus our attention on the "here and now". We bring what we learn from the "who" identifying starting points and apply what we learn in the present. While we don't forget the past we shouldn't spend most of our time trying to relive the past or rectify every unfinished area in our past. When we do that we end up missing out on what is happening in our relationships right now. We miss the important clues, warning signs, and even amazing moments in the right now because we spend entirely too much time looking back on our past. The future is also very important and shouldn't be ignored but, again, spending too much time trying to figure out what the future will look like will have us developing too many "rigid expectations". These expectations will cause us to lose focus on the relationship in the here and now and we will miss out on the accomplishments that are happening right before our eyes. It has been my experience that no one wins in trying to reach expectations that are unchanging and leave no room for us to grow, to make mistakes, to forgive, and eventually evaluate what direction we may need to go in our relationships.

Love with Balance is the fourth starting point and is very important. I have learned that, besides getting over me, which was very difficult for me to do, I was also very unbalanced in my relationships and I got lost in this unbalanced way of relating to others that I thought was normal. This starting point is very essential to fully implementing the new principles of loving yourself and others that I hope you gain from reading this book.

Love Me Right or Not At All

Balance is an incredible yet very under used tool in our arsenal to help make relationships work and work effectively. If I just applied balance from the start of every relationship I entered I possibly would have been spared the unnecessary heartache and pain that came from such unstable ways of loving. If this is the only place you feel you need to start, please do so with an open mind and truly identify where you may need to create balance in your journey toward healthy relationships. Balance is key to loving yourself right, loving others the right way, and loving others right in the here and now. I have been incredibly free in the last few months by applying these principles before I even knew I was going to write them and share them. I hope that you start at one or all of these starting points and obtain the freedom that I have now, but let it be experienced in a way that is uniquely yours. Please enjoy this journey to discovering how to love yourself and others the right way.

STARTING POINT 1: GET OVER YOURSELF

Take off the Mask

As simple as this starting point sounds, this is possibly the most difficult thing to do in changing your perspective of relationships. I asked myself, when I was experiencing my reset and evaluative moment, "How in the world will I get over myself?" and I was totally afraid to do it. I felt that, if I let go of who I created myself to be, I would be lost. I didn't want to lose the person that I created myself to be. I didn't want to lose the lies that I had told about myself. I took every negative thing that people had said about me, every flaw that people pointed out about me, every flaw that I saw within myself; I took these thoughts and perspectives and created a mask and built myself up. It seemed like an excellent idea at the time, not to let people keep me down or become what people said I was, but I made myself into this amazing person who didn't take anything from anyone. To be quite honest, I became a slightly pessimistic, guarded, and paranoid person who took these fears, beliefs, and destructive behavior patterns into my relationships.

I bottled all these things up and viewed the people I was in relationship with, not as lovers or friends, but as people I couldn't live without, as well as people I could not let hurt me. I had great qualities—faithful, honest, romantic, funny, and caring—but these qualities were buried in my desire to protect myself and were overshadowed by my desire to please others. I found myself in a cycle of bad relationships and I was becoming very toxic from inhaling all of the negative fumes that I brought into these relationships. I was also ignoring all of the poison that others were bringing into my life as well. Have you ever felt like you were drowning in your own mess? This was the overwhelming burden that I had placed on myself first and I then allowed others to add their weights on to the heavy chains I placed on myself.

Love Me Right or Not At All

I got so lost in the façade of being "real" that I was unable to tell when I was being fake or when the people around me didn't have my best interests at heart. I became lost in a false sense of truthfulness that any real truth someone told me made me withdraw from them or regard them as "haters". I made it worse by blaming others and never putting in the work to fix me. I worked so hard at keeping my mask on and trying to fix others that I was no longer able to tell that I was broken and didn't really love who I truly was. I became too afraid to let people see the vulnerable me and it did nothing but cast me further away from finding true and healthy love. This negatively affected my relationships across the board: at home, at work, with friends, and with family. I can't even describe in full detail how this unhealthy way of living affected intimate relationships, but I can tell you this—it was not pretty. I lied to myself about "who" I was and attempted to make myself into the person I wanted to be.

Love Me Right or Not At All

This may not be your story and you might not agree with this, but I know that most people who read this will need to get over themselves in order to move forward in relationships. This book is about loving yourself first in a healthy way so that you can effectively love others in a healthy way as well. <u>You can't do that wearing a mask</u> and you definitely can't do that <u>believing the lies you tell yourself</u>. We believe that living our lies is very difficult; day in and day out trying to convince people we are who we say we are. Most of us struggle daily to fight who we were meant to be, against who we desire to be, against what people say we are. We never fully reach what psychologist Abraham Maslow described as, "self-actualization." How can we reach our actualized selves when we have no idea who we are? How can we begin to love another person platonically or romantically when we can't even love ourselves? The difficulty isn't in wearing the masks, it is our habits. The masks are our nature; the difficulty is in removing the mask.

Love Me Right or Not At All

Removing the mask will expose the real you and it will also make you vulnerable. In reality that is what you need in order to truly have your reset moment: "The Real You". I honestly believed that I wasn't bitter or angry, that I could forgive all the wrongs people had done to me; I believed that I could be in a relationship with anyone I desired, and that I could make even the most unhealthiest relationship work. I believed people <u>owed me</u> something because of all the pain others caused me, especially in relationships. I wanted to show people that I was strong and that, no matter how far you kicked me to the ground, I would stand back up. Then I discovered that, with all of this power and all the affirmations I could give myself, I was OK, and I was ready to love other people. I believed that the person I created was ready to be in a successful relationship, which would one day lead to marriage and children; I convinced myself that I didn't have to address the hurt, the guilt, or the shame that I buried so deep within myself. My mask was formed and firmly in place. I would love harder and better than anyone

Love Me Right or Not At All

else. I would make it hard for the next person to ever be able to step in and take my place. I would be the best husband any woman could ever ask for. So if all of this was in place, why were my relationships still failing? Why did just about every relationship last no more than three to six months? Why did I fall so hard for people I'd only been dating for a month or so? There are a number of factors why my relationships failed, but after I stopped and truly evaluated myself I learned that I was not ready for a relationship. I wasn't ready to be in a healthy relationship because I was an unhealthy individual who wasn't over himself, and who was still wearing a mask. In order for you to love someone else the right way you must first get over yourself and take off the mask.

STARTING POINT 1: GET OVER YOURSELF

Let Go Of The Past You

I told you from the beginning that getting over yourself was going to be a process and for some of us a much more difficult process than we want to believe. However, we must remove the mask that hides who we really are and remove the mask that has buried our pain and hurts. Once we are free from our masked self, it is time for us to let go of our past self. I know it may seem harsh or even counterproductive to tell yourself that you are not that important or you're not all that, but, truthfully, this type of self-talk will have you overconfident or arrogant to the point where you're unable to see clearly. You are unable to see that you are still very much wounded and hurt by your past, that you haven't recovered from the lost friendships, family hurt, and even the failed relationships. We take all that encompasses our past self and we hide it behind the mask. We take this "person" and we squeeze them behind a wall of "confidence", "arrogance" or "our guarded self". We take this person and we bring them into our relationships. If this isn't you, congratulations, but if it is let's continue to explore how to change this state of being.

    We should not make our friends, family, or significant others pay for our past mistakes or the errors of those who hurt or harmed us. This happens a lot in relationships and most times we are unaware that it is happening. We push the people who truly care for us away because we have not acknowledged our pain or we haven't acknowledged that we did people wrong; there has been no acceptance that we made poor decisions in our past, or we continue to push the blame on to other people. It is difficult to have a successful relationship if we live in our past or we still live as our past selves. Sometimes we feel that if we forget our past life we will repeat the past and we will be hurt all over again, but if we bring our past into our present relationships, people won't want to be around us or in relationships with us. I'm not asking you to forget the hurt of your past or to forget how you overcame that pain. I don't want you to forget, but I want you to free yourself from it. Don't live out your past in your future. Your past should not be your focus point; your focus should be on a healthy sense of your present self. We will talk a little more about focusing on the here and now in later chapters, but letting go of your past self is the next step in fully getting over yourself. When you are fully over yourself you can begin to focus on loving yourself in a healthy way and concentrate on loving others in a healthy way as well.

Again, I don't want this to be a bash-yourself party and I am not telling you to put yourself down, but I am saying that you have to come to the realization that you are not all that. To get over yourself you have to face the fact that no one owes you anything! This is vital to letting go of your past self; we make the mistake of holding on to hurts and wrongs because we feel that someone owes us an apology or that we should be treated like royalty because we went through something. This isn't intended to minimize the hurt, pain, or trauma that you may have endured, but I am writing this to help us all realize that you can't ignore the work that needs to be done to heal because you are waiting for someone to ask you for your forgiveness or to make up for all the pain you went through.

Let's just say that you've never been hurt and this sense of entitlement is an indication that you are either detached from the thoughts and feelings of others and enamored with your own wants and needs, or it is an indication of some sort of personality disorder; if you have this belief that you are owed something, it is time to let that go. No matter what the source is, feelings of entitlement will only cause you to behave inappropriately in relationships, and push people away. It is not your family, friends, or your partner's responsibility to pay for your past. If you place this expectation on them then I'm sorry to say either you'll be by yourself or you will continue on the path of unhealthy relationships. This cycle will not end until you can make the decision to let go of your past self and not take your past into your relationships.

"How do I let go of my past self?" It starts with realizing that you are not all that, no one owes you anything, and that you deserve to love yourself first. It is no longer OK to be overconfident or arrogant. Remember this book is all about being a healthy you and loving someone in a healthy way. It is OK to be confident, as long as you have dealt with your fears, flaws, and issues in a healthy and realistic way. Confidence is healthy. Overconfidence, however, is often a byproduct of insecurities and hurts that have not been addressed and oftentimes is an indication that we still have on our masks.

Arrogance is not just a state of being or a way of thinking, it is involved in overly selfish motives that produce self-pleasuring actions. Arrogance is the ultimate display that "I am a gift to you," "I am all that matters," and "You owe me everything." If you are arrogant you may be unhealthy and doing relationships in a very unhealthy way. The key reason for the starting point

Get Over Yourself is not to put people down, but to identify unhealthy ways of thinking about yourself and implementing the appropriate changes needed to love yourself the healthy way. It is OK to have high self-esteem or even be confident in who you are, or confident in how you look, but letting confidence get in the way of the work that needs to be done is unhealthy. Arrogance is not only unhealthy, but, after a while, even the people who find your arrogance attractive will begin to become annoyed by it. Checking you and putting yourself in place will help you decide which thoughts, feelings, and behaviors need to be removed from your life, and what strengths you have that may need to be amplified. This is all for the sake of being healthy. I went through these steps and I know that it can be a major hit to hear someone tell you that you have to get over yourself. It is hard to hear, hard to read, and even harder to implement, but I can assure you of this—you will heal. When you let go of your past and you deal with your hurts and insecurities, you begin to feel free. All I wanted was to love who

I was and not worry about what others thought about me. I approached this in a very unhealthy way and was somewhat successful for a little while. This engendered short-lived success and I realized that I had to put in the hard work to truly be free and truly love who I am.

Are you willing to do the work to let go of the past you so that you can have a healthy you today? Are you willing to truly address the things that you have bottled up so that you can move forward into a healthy love with yourself and healthy love with others? As I said, reading this book will mean nothing if you can't take the starting points outlined in this book and apply them in a way that works for you and the people that you are in relationship with. It is unfair to everyone you enter into relationship with to expect them to pay for your past self. It is very unfair for you to ask someone to love the unhealthy you just the way you are. It is unfair to believe that others have to make changes to accommodate your madness or insecurities when you have no plans to change who you are. What is the point of holding on to your past if it ruins your future? Let go of the mask that hides the real you and let go of the past you that is negatively affecting your present relationships.

STARTING POINT 1: GET OVER YOURSELF

Give of Yourself and Not Give To Yourself in Relationships

If you have made it this far without putting the book down, or maybe this chapter just called out to you, I want to tell you that I am proud of you. I am proud that you have continued reading because it is not easy to be told, to accept, or even acknowledge that we may need to get over ourselves in order to have successful relationships. As I stated before, we are on this journey together. I have had to get over myself, get over my past, and accept that there are some things that I need to let go so that I can become a healthy person and have healthy relationships. I want the same for you and your relationships. So if you have not removed the mask, take it off right now. There is no reason for you to continue to hide behind who you're not just to make other people happy or so as not to deal with the mess that you may be. It is time to accept who you are, it is time to work on the things that limit you from reaching your full potential, and it is time to let go of the lies that you have told yourself. Take off the mask and let go of the past you.

Yes, let go of the past you because it isn't helping you in your present relationships and if your past was full of anger, lies, hurt, and fears, why would you think it would be helpful to hold on to it? How will holding on to your "past self" help you in your future? I'm not telling you to forget the past, but I am saying don't hold on to something that has done nothing put poison your perspective, made you distrustful, or has you so completely guarded that no one can come in. It is not OK to have someone pay for the mistakes of others. It is not acceptable to let your present relationships suffer because of what you lacked or what was taken from you in your past relationships. If you want to get to healthy and have healthy relationships you have to let go of the past you. Take whatever you need from the past to help you avoid making the same mistakes, but holding onto grudges, bitterness, and pain is not the way to move forward. Blaming and self-doubt because you continue to look through the lens of your past is not the way to have a healthy present or a healthy future. Your past is just that, your past; let it go and move forward.

Now that you have let go of your masked self and your past self, it is time to Give of Yourself and Not Give to Yourself in moving towards loving yourself and others the right way. We are moving towards becoming a healthier person; we are becoming the true and real version of ourselves that has been hidden behind lies and hurt. In doing so we must now recognize that there is a level of selfishness that must be addressed and dealt with in order to become our healthy selves. This involves understanding that the people in relationships have to learn to give themselves to their friends or significant other and allow those people to give themselves back in return. A large number of us are stuck in the me, myself, and I phase when we enter into relationships or we look through the lens of give to me, love me, fix me, help me, do for me, pray for me, build me up, pleasure me; we feel that those that we are in relationship with must do this or they don't love us. We feel that if they don't constantly meet our needs the way we want them met something is wrong with them and the relationship. This is a breeding ground for selfishness and resentment that will end relationships. This is accelerated if we have on a mask, lying to our significant others about who we really are, and we are making them pay for our past; this causes us to only want things done for ourselves, or we will only do for them when they do for us. This is no way to do relationships and why it is important that we work on ourselves first and love ourselves first so we can love others the right way.

It is OK to desire that your significant other or your friends meet your needs. This is one of the main reasons that we enter into relationships, so that we can get our needs met that we may not be able to meet ourselves. Getting your needs met isn't the issue that I want to address, but it is the selfish desire to only get our own needs met in our relationships, or only being motivated to meet the needs of others if yours are met exactly the way you want them to be. It is about balance, balance is something we will talk about in detail in later chapters, but to have a healthy relationship there should be an even balance of both individuals meeting each other's needs. This chapter, however, is about fixing yourself first and how we should learn to be willing to give of ourselves and not just become fixated on our needs being met and met alone. We have to work not to become so lost in our own wants and needs getting met that we forget to meet the needs of our loved ones. If we are consumed with getting our own needs met we become blind to the needs of those who we are in relationship with; relationship blindness becomes habitual for us, and we are unable to see how neglected and possibly overwhelmed our loved ones are trying to meet our needs while their own needs go unmet.

We may be further blinded by the fact that the needs that we want met may not be reasonable and those we love become resentful and unwilling to try to meet our needs. That's why it is so important that we change our perspective on how to love not just by loving ourselves first, but by giving of ourselves willingly and unselfishly to those who are willing to give to us. Again, I will talk more about who to give ourselves to in later chapters, but I want to be clear that we should be giving and receiving. We say and believe that we give in our relationships, but many times it is contingent upon our needs being met first, or the intent is, "If I give them this then I should receive that." That line of thinking still keeps us in the give to yourself attitude and will possibly leave you and your spouse with unmet needs and frustration.

A healthy you can give to others and not require anything in return. This sounds really crazy to a lot of people because we are told it is better to give than receive, but we are taught to give if it is given to us. We learn and act on the behavior we are shown, rather than what we are told. This is why in relationships we live by the mentality, "If they do something for me then I will do something for them." This can be a very unhealthy way of doing relationships and is often the reason why a lot of relationships end. We have that give and take perspective and we are often detached from what others are doing for us, fixated on what appears they aren't doing for us, and we are unappreciative of the things they have given us. In order to love and love the right way you must strive to be a healthy you in all ways possible. It starts with you deciding, "I can appreciate what people do for me, I can give without them having to give to me, and I can honestly be comfortable with giving and have no requirements for a return." We have to get over ourselves and remember that no one owes us anything. If we are still living in the stage of self-gratification and self-indulgence we are hindering ourselves from being loving and appreciative of those we love and those who love us.

Ask yourself this question, "Do you want to be a healthy you?" What is the answer to this question? Hopefully, after reading up to this point, you have come to understand what a healthy you should look like. It is a very difficult thing to

Love Me Right or Not At All

unmask yourself and then change the way you have been doing things. It could possibly be a very painful process, but think of the healthy you that you can become. It is an incredibly powerful ability to give to others and not have the burden of expecting something in return. You free yourself from disappointment, heartache, and frustration when you give from a genuine place in your heart; you give and it is not clouded by being upset that you didn't get anything from them.

STARTING POINT 1: GET OVER YOURSELF

Embrace the New You

For some of us this starting point may have been easy, because we aren't that into ourselves, we just needed a little evaluation to get back on the right track; for the rest of us this starting point may have really caused us some trouble. We had to dig very deep to let go of years of anger, frustration, and hurt. There was a lot of work and effort put into tearing down the protective walls that we put up and getting the painful mask off of our faces. This process may have caused lots of pain and scarring; don't worry, we are now going to work on healing from the letting go process, and we are going to embrace the new you. That's right; now that we have a healthy love for ourselves, it is time for us to begin to embrace who we are, and start the journey of loving ourselves the right way, loving ourselves the healthy way. It is all about being healthy and balanced in the love we have for ourselves. We do not believe the lies people have said about us and we are not going to believe the lies we have told ourselves. At this moment we are embracing the new, free, and unmasked version of ourselves. We are accepting that we are free, unmasked, living in our truth; we have let go of the past, we aren't making people pay for the mistakes of others, we are giving of ourselves, and we are safely navigating loving ourselves in a healthy way. I don't want you to be afraid to love yourself. A healthy self-esteem is not synonymous with arrogance or an inflated ego.

    We must first begin healing from the exposure. We often have difficulty going through the healing process. We get counseling, we get advice from our pastor, or we get great support from our friends; we hurt and we cry, but we do not let what we learned sink in and we don't embrace the process of healing. So I want us to not only embrace the new person we are aiming to become, but I want us to embrace healing from the exposure that unmasking ourselves will cause. Think about what healing from a bad cut or burn is like. Think about how much time it takes for the pain to stop, for the new skin to grow, and how the body helps you adjust both physically and mentally from the trauma of being exposed to pain and suffering. I believe that this is the same for mental and emotional pain as well. As I said, this starting point was going to make us work and letting go of our mental and emotional baggage in order to get over ourselves may have caused a lot of cuts, scrapes, and bruises. The mask that was embedded so deeply and hiding who you truly were was fused to your skin. Could you imagine what it must feel like to remove something that was fused and fixed tightly on your face?

The process of healing is necessary because the exposure is going to hurt. The air is going to hit your raw skin and it will burn. The way people will look at and may even judge you will hurt so badly, but we will discuss how to deal with those people in later chapters so don't worry about them right now. I'm asking that you begin to heal from the exposure by refusing to pick at the scabs or interrupt the healing process.

Picking at a scab will only interrupt the healing process and, believe me, we will be tempted to go back to our old way of life. We were so comfortable being so into ourselves, getting validation from others, and hiding behind our masks that coming out into the light feels painful and we do not recognize the scabs that are all over the once exposed, rather hidden, skin. Some of us believe that the scabs aren't a part of the healing process, but rather an ill reminder that we were hurt and we don't want to be reminded of our hurt or what we had to let go. The honest truth is scabs aren't beautiful, but their unattractive look often hides a powerful purpose.

Honestly, healing is never a beautiful process. The scab provides protection and allows your body's defenses to fight things that don't belong there. Scabs protect the new skin that is forming underneath it and keeps the negativity out. Don't pick the scab or interrupt the healing process so that you can remain protected. A large portion of us as human beings are very impatient and do not want to go through any process that we may deem is too long or doesn't give us immediate results. We have to work very hard not to rush the process of healing because we will find ourselves back in pain and trying to get back to our old comfort zone. I truly believe that a lot of us are stuck at this point in our process of healing and maturity, because we can't stop picking the scabs. We constantly remind ourselves of our shortcomings, our inadequacies, or we ruminate over the negative things people have said about us. We spend too much time in our feelings of sadness, loneliness, or self-hatred, turning these feelings into something more powerful, "reality". We defeat any progress that we have made toward becoming a whole person or embracing the new "us"; when we destroy the scabs because they don't look attractive or feel beautiful, we find ourselves right back in the beginning.

    Healing from the exposure is going to take time, but it requires that we don't constantly pick at the scabs. Even if we

Love Me Right or Not At All

enjoy picking at the scabs, we have to resist the urge to do so. We have to let the scabs do their job and heal us. Remember picking at the scabs only interrupts the healing process and prolongs the process of embracing the new you.

STARTING POINT 2: LOVE YOURSELF NOW

Why Love Myself after You Told Me to Get over Myself?

Getting over yourself and loving yourself are two completely different things, but both are affected by the way we think of ourselves. I wanted us to move from being unhealthy to being healthy, but I knew that going through that process was going to be challenging. Right now, if you took all the steps, did all the work, and really removed the mask, you are either healing or you are not very happy with what has been exposed. Some of us want to go back to who we were, we want to go back to the lies we told ourselves and the lies others have told to us because we were comfortable. Any change is very difficult and, oftentimes, when the truth is exposed we are not in love with or happy about this new person we are. That's why I want us to love who we are now and to let go of who we were.

Love Me Right or Not At All

    As I stated in the first chapter, this starting point is one that focuses on the here and now perspective. In other words, it helps us to focus on the present and not the past. Many times we get so lost in trying to escape our past, or living in it, that we miss out on what is currently happening. We miss out on important things that are transpiring in our current situation and then we end up confused as to why people are upset with us or why no one wants us around. The reason for this forced isolation is that the people you're around are aware that you are not present and that you are stuck in the past. This starting point will help us focus on the right now! Right now I love who I am! I'm not focusing on my potential, but on what I have to bring to the table right at this moment. You may be starting here first and you may work your way backwards, but if you skipped the first starting point then your focus right now is to love who you are! It is time to forget everything you didn't do and to fully focus on what you can do right at this moment.

Love Me Right or Not At All

What are your strengths? What are your limitations? Yes, you have to embrace both your strengths and limitations because they make you who you are. Notice that I said limitations and not weaknesses. Limitations can be turned into strengths. Limitations also teach us boundaries and restraints that are often absent in individuals who are either too into themselves or individuals who are stuck looking into the past. Truly take the time to identify what you love about yourself and present those things to the people you are in relationship with. Oftentimes we have put so much time and effort into becoming the person other people wanted us to be. We spent years idolizing and envying someone else and we fell out of love with the unique person that we were created to be. This line of thinking has contributed heavily to our beliefs in societal labels, jealousy, and hatred towards people we think are better than we are. That's why it is so important that we change our focus and look at loving the person we are. If you know that you can't love who you are right at this moment, we must work on it right now!

Love Me Right or Not At All

In order to start loving yourself the healthy way in the here and now, we have to Reset, Rethink, Revive, and Resurface. In many instances, we set goals and resolutions, but we did not plan, we did not evaluate those plans, assess whether those plans would work; we did not get motivated or bring those plans back to life when they died; and we did not implement the goals we set. This is why we often feel stuck or get stuck in our past because we keep starting over with the same clutter and garbage we didn't throw away and never truly give ourselves a clean slate or a true starting over point. So we have to reset ourselves, start with a fresh plan or new set of goals. To fall back in love with who we are, we need a fresh perspective on just who we are, and what we need to love about ourselves.

When we hit the reset button we have to make sure that we take full advantage of the clearing process that a reset gives to us. You get a clean slate, you get to add or subtract from the first time around, and you get to start at the beginning with a new mindset. We truly need to take advantage of the reset button when we decide to press it. Once you throw away all the negativity or the garbage, the procrastination, the broken promises, and the self-hatred, you throw that all away and now you have a chance to start over and plan again. Let's set realistic goals for ourselves and let us work hard to identify what we can excel at. Take this reset and focus on setting goals that build you up as a person, take opportunities to invest in yourself, and truly take the time to embrace learning from your mistakes. After the reset, it is now time to rethink.

Rethinking your plan, goals, or strategy is vital to the process of learning to love yourself now. Sometimes we just jump right into the first plan that we develop and we run with it. We don't really take the time to look and understand if this is the best way to go, if our goals are realistic, measurable, and obtainable. When we just jump straight into the first plan of action, we may miss some very important details. Then, if we fail, we don't take the option to reset and start over, but since we are on the path to loving who we are right now and right at this moment, take this time to rethink your plans. Rethinking involves us evaluating and assessing what is going on, where we want to go, and how we are going to get there. To rethink is to look at the plan we developed before the reset happened, rethink the plan that we developed after the reset happened, and to even create and develop an additional plan or follow up plan just in case things don't work out again. Loving yourself now is going to take a lot of work because we may have spent so much time avoiding who we are, lying about who we are, or listening to what others said we should be or shouldn't be doing. However, this is your chance to rethink all of those things, to start afresh and to take control of what your next steps are going to be.

What I want you to grasp from this point is not only do you need to love yourself right now, but you have to plan to do everything in your power to build yourself up presently so that you'll have a future to look forward to. <u>We get so impatient with ourselves</u>. We want everything to happen in an instant. It took time, however, for you to jump in and out of bad relationships; it took time for our marriages to become rocky or dysfunctional; it took a long time for us to forget about all the positive things we have within us, all of the strengths, all the positive things that were taught to us; it took time to do damage, so why do we want to rush the healing? The rethinking step gives us that time to truly fall in love with the new us. In the previous starting point we had to get over ourselves, but then we had to embrace the new us. We have already looked into our past and I know we are eager to peek into our future, but we must focus on what is happening right now and right at this moment. We should take a deeper look into what we are feeling now.

Did you really take the time to embrace the new you? Did you live in the emotions of setting yourself free from your past and your past hurts? Did you take time to understand what your reset was really all about? This is why rethinking is so vital to this process. Rethinking gives you an opportunity to look at the directions you have set and make sure that this is the right way to go. Loving yourself now can't happen if you still refuse to believe that the new you is real and that this new person can move forward in a healthy way. This is often the battle for a lot of us who believe that Jesus Christ is the Son of God and the sacrifice he gave to us is real and the freedom it gives is real. After we get saved, we don't always walk in our freedom, or we dive right into our reset; we dive in and we have a good stride, but, because of poor planning, we end up right back in bondage. This is also how we end up back in the same unhealthy relationship patterns. We get out of a terrible or unhealthy relationship and we say, "I will never go back to something like that," but because we still operate in the previous plan, we end up right back in the same unhealthy or dysfunctional relationship because we refused to rethink our plans.

Take all the time you need to develop, assess, and evaluate your goals and plans. Assessment lets you know what you need and where you want to go. Evaluation allows you to not only look at what you have assessed, but also to see what has worked and what hasn't; it allows you to add and subtract as you go.

Rethink your goals and plans through assessment and evaluation. If that process becomes tedious or frustrating, or if you made a solid plan but grew exhausted from all the work it took to plan, it may be time for you to revive the plan.

Revive your plans, your goals, and your dreams. This is such an important step for a lot us out there who are not only trying to learn to love ourselves, but also how we can truly learn to love others in a healthy way. I do understand that I am skipping ahead, but I want to address the power that comes from loving yourself first but also the power that can come when you truly understand how to love others in a healthy way. We are often our greatest enemies. We are often the first to put ourselves down, we are the first to limit ourselves, we are the first to accept and live out the negative things people have said about us; we do this before they even get a chance to feed us that garbage. We do this and we allow our hopes and dreams to die. How many unfinished books do we have? How many proposals do we have piled up or buried away in clutter? How many tears have we cried because we have sabotaged our dreams or destroyed relationships that were good for us and meant something to us? How many times have we promised God, our friends, our families, or our significant others that we were going to start over, do better, or chase after our dreams only to let those dreams die? This is why so many of us are unable to love who we are right now; we are unable to do it because we are covered in the dirt of the graves we built for ourselves.

    We can't move towards loving who we are because we only see ourselves in our grave clothes; we only see ourselves in our attire of bondage. If this is what is holding you back from loving yourself right now, it is time to unbury yourself, take off the grave clothes; remove the things that have you trapped and revive your goals, hopes, and dreams. To revive the love you have for yourself and to revive the goals and plans you have created for the new you, you have to become motivated to start working towards your goals and bring back to life the positive things that have died and been buried underneath hurt, guilt, and shame. To become motivated, you will need to surround yourself with positive people, places, and things. <u>Stop hanging around in graveyards trying to find life</u>. Get in a space or several spaces that empower you, which illuminates your passions, which stimulates your mind, and will allow you to see yourself as a living being that is full of possibilities. We try to maintain a healthy relationship with someone in a dysfunctional space. Your environment plays a part in shaping your relationships and how you view yourself.

We try so hard to just be around people that we miss the fact that the people we are around are zombies. Here again, you are trying to revive your hopes and dreams, trying your hardest to love yourself and rebuild yourself, but you are around people who enjoy seeing you fail and around people who feed off of your pain and misery. We spend so much time trying to stay around people who enjoy seeing us in our graves. You can't revive anything positive hanging around people who love being the living dead. As I already said, I am getting ahead of myself and I will discuss in later chapters the people we need to be around, but I wanted to be clear that you can't take the next step in loving yourself now and revive your goals and dreams if you continue to be around negative people. Even the things we have in our lives can cause us to remain dead. Some of us are in the same jobs, friending zombie-like people on different social media sites, using the same computers, phones, or emails that have housed all of the negativity that has kept us from loving who we are and looking back at where we failed.

I can't write this enough; you can't <u>revive</u> anything if you keep the same negative people, places, and things in your life. To become motivated to bring your hopes and dreams back to life you have to surround yourself with positive people, places, and things. It may be time to invest in a new computer or a new phone that can do bigger and better things; that isn't tied to a past relationship. Maybe you can't move or afford to move to a new space, but you can set a new atmosphere in the place that you are in so that you can control the energy that is surrounding you.

Listen, loving yourself now means that you have some work to do beyond getting over yourself or taking off the mask. You are going to try to put yourself back in that box of unhealthiness and bury yourself in failure, guilt, shame, hatred, paranoia, isolation, depression; you will be tempted to do so, but if you remember that you have already hit the rest button on your life and that you have been rethinking your plan, you can come out of this pit and start reviving your hopes and dreams. You can bring back to life all the things that meant something to you. You can revive the positive relationships that you were in and you can shape your environments into living and positive spaces that will help you live and help you revive the things that are going to assist you with loving yourself now. Once you have revived yourself, your goals, and dreams, the time has come for you to dig yourself out of that negative grave and resurface.

Love Me Right or Not At All

Resurface is the final step in the process. This chapter has a subtitle of "Why Love Myself after You Told Me to Get over Myself?" I don't think I have fully taken the time to answer that question. I want you to begin to love yourself because, in my opinion, besides God, no one is going to be able to love you just for who you are—flaws, problems, issues, strengths, and limitations—but you! It is absolutely unrealistic for us to expect someone other than God Himself to love each and everything about us, but it is also unrealistic for us to expect God and other people to love us when we don't even love ourselves. You can't move forward if you don't love you and especially love the new you—absent a mask and absent the things you used to hide about yourself. We have to resurface because we buried ourselves again. Moving forward with our revived hopes, goals, and dreams requires that we uncover ourselves from going back to dead places, strengthening what motivates us, and implementing the goals and objectives we have set. Once we

Love Me Right or Not At All

realize that it is up to us to love ourselves first, flaws and all, this is the only way that we can fully embrace loving others.

I wanted you to get over yourself so that you can fully embrace this new mindset of loving yourself. Sometimes we use so much energy putting ourselves down, blaming others for our insecurities, and ignoring the hurt and pain that we have not addressed that we end up buried under all of this mess. Now that you have let go of the old you, you can resurface and put into action loving yourself first, implementing the steps to reach whatever goals you have set for yourself, and start the journey of loving people the right way. To do this we have to give ourselves permission to move forward, to let go of all of the weights that have kept us defeated and walk in freedom. We can only begin to resurface when we see ourselves as individuals deserving to be revived, renewed, and refreshed. If we still spend so much time on where we fail, where we're weak, and what we don't have, we have not gotten over ourselves. Without hitting the reset button, we will be stuck in the same cycle of unhealthy relationships; the cycle of an unhealthy relationship with ourselves and a cycle of unhealthy relationships with others.

We don't have to stay in that cycle! We can resurface and begin to implement the goals and changes we have set from the moment we took off our masks and hit the reset button. Resurfacing is going to take work, but think about how much stronger you will be after you have dug yourself out of that hole. Will you be tempted to stay buried beneath guilt and shame? Will you be tempted to revert back to your old self and your old ways? Will you feel as though it is easier to focus only on what people don't do for you rather than focusing on how you can love yourself better? The answer to all of these questions is yes! You will find yourself sometimes wishing you could stay behind the mask or be able to focus on the past. It took time to develop bad habits and breaking them will take time as well. However, if you have reached the point of resurfacing, you are saying that you are ready to move forward. You have hit your reset button

Love Me Right or Not At All

and developed a new plan. You have evaluated and reassessed your plan and situation. You may have had some setbacks or you may have gone back to your old way of living, but you recognize that you have the power to revive yourself and bring back to life the plans you have made to better yourself. Now that you have taken these steps it is time for you to resurface and get to work on moving forward.

STARTING POINT 2: LOVE YOURSELF NOW

Look Forward and Only Look Back to Avoid Repeating the Past

It can be challenging to love yourself when people constantly remind you of who you used to be. The difficulty increases when you're the one reminding yourself of your failures, your heartache, and the setbacks that you have faced in the past. A healthy relationship can't be formed when an individual is trying to live in two different mindsets or perspectives. It is important that we focus on what is currently happening in our lives, to truly look at how we can be involved in what is happening right now and right at this moment. It is detrimental to continue to live in the past because we are trying to fix things that can't be changed. To spend so much time in the past, we end up ignoring the person we are, the people who are with us, and we lose sight of the direction we are going in. You can't love you if you are held back by what happened in your past. As described in the first starting point, you have to get over yourself and you have to get over your past. You don't owe your past or your past mistakes anything. You have already paid the price for your mistakes, you have already faced the consequences, or you have already regretted what you have done. It is now time to resolve what has been left unfinished in your past and move forward. We are impairing a healthy love for ourselves and a detriment to a healthy relationship with others if we are stuck in the past, or if we are stuck in what happened in our past.

Looking forward is the mind set of individuals who understand that they are physically, spiritually, emotionally, mentally, and literally unable to change any aspect of their past. You look forward to strengthen your resolve to become the strongest version of yourself, the most successful version of yourself; you are looking forward so that you can avoid the mistakes of your past and set up a better future for yourself.

Love Me Right or Not At All

Looking forward takes courage. It is often a very scary thing to move forward without wondering about your past. What good has it been for you and your relationships to dwell on your past? You are looking forward to a new beginning because you have come to the realization that you don't have to be bound by your past. I am not making any excuses for any wrong you may have done, you need to deal with any unresolved issues in your past, but you don't have to dwell in your past and let it shape your future. You can look forward because you have taken off the mask that kept you hidden from truth and light, you have begun the healing process, and you're enjoying the experience of being free. If your focus is on letting it all go and you have started the journey of loving yourself now, are resetting, rethinking, reviving, and resurfacing, you're doing all of this, how do you have any time to look into your past?

Hasn't that been exhausting for you? What do you get out of thinking about everything someone did to you or didn't do for you? What good comes from constantly thinking of your failures and convincing yourself you don't deserve to move forward? Moving forward is difficult because we are not over ourselves and we believe that if we look forward we will no longer have control. If we forgive the people who have wronged us in our past we believe that they have won and we have relinquished power over to them. This is not true! We are taking control and retaking our power when we let go of the past and let go of the people in it as well.

We should be looking forward to doing bigger and better things, and only look back to avoid repeating the past. Looking back should be a quick glance if something comes your way that looks or feels familiar. Our past is our history, but history often repeats itself. In the moments when history is trying to repeat itself, take a look back only to grasp the points that look familiar and use that to avoid repeating past mistakes. When you begin to love yourself and you embrace the new you, your past is going to try to dissuade you from moving forward. You will believe that you are not worthy of a second chance or another chance

Love Me Right or Not At All

and you'll go back to feeling sorry for yourself and become unable to respond to the good that is with you now. We lose connections with the right people and the right environments because we are stuck in what has happened in the past. We miss out on what is good for us and who is right for us because we are focused on all the bad that has happened to us and are absent to the good that is currently happening. Stop looking into the past and embrace the right now.

STARTING POINT 2: LOVE YOURSELF NOW!

Remove past People from Your Present Life

Loving yourself is going to take you understanding who needs to be in your life and who doesn't. Starting point number three will discuss Give Love to the Right People, but I wanted to take some time right now to let you know that letting go of your past means letting go of some people in your past as well. As hard as it is to admit, not everyone is meant to be in your life. We spend too much time speaking and living in absolutes. We use always and never in our relationships and we believe that they would never betray us and they will always be in our lives. There are some people who aren't meant to be with you forever and, honestly, they shouldn't have been in your life in the first place. Oftentimes we do learn how to love ourselves and encourage ourselves, but there is something or rather someone who continues to hold you back and keep you in your past. What is twisted is that you **know** who is from your past and who is holding you back, but you are so blindly loyal you refuse to see that this individual or these people don't mean you well. They drain you and they refuse to allow you to forget your past because they understand very clearly that, if you let go of your past, their control over you will diminish.

You have to be empowered and encouraged to remove those people from your past who don't belong in your present. Notice that I did not say let them go. Letting them go would be too passive, instead you have to take an assertive role in your own life and remove them from your present life and let them live in your past. These individuals are the ones who not only understand your past and what hurts you, but they know what buttons to push. The people in your past have spent a great deal of time studying what moves you and what hurts you, so they'll know exactly how to get what they want out of you. They are often the individuals who not only wear masks themselves, but

Love Me Right or Not At All

they helped superglue the mask you once wore so that it would stay fixed to your face. That is why you have to remove them from your present life. They are not ever going to want you to do well. It is their desire to have you staying in the same sad state because they aren't healthy or renewed. You know who the past people are because they are the ones who are right there at your lowest point under the pretense they are there to support, but everything out of their mouth is what you can't do or a constant reminder of how you failed to do better in your past. They are either consistently present to see what you are doing or they are inconsistent in their communication but expect you to do all the work to keep the relationship intact. If you have healthy self-esteem and you have begun to reap the benefits of loving who you are, you will quickly notice the people in your past who don't need to be with you now. It is time to take them by the hand and place them in the past where they belong.

    I want to stop at this moment and say that there is no need to become paranoid. I don't want you to believe everyone is out to get you or out to hurt you. If you are feeling this way or starting to feel like you are being targeted, your past self is trying to creep back in, and your mask is trying to fix itself back on your face. Those paranoid thoughts are an indication that you may be starting to get too involved with yourself. Remember you're not doing this to satisfy some superiority complex. No one is beneath us; we aren't better than anyone else. The work that needs to be done is taking control over who is in our lives and how those interactions shape us either positively or negatively. We have let so many unnecessary situations affect us and shape who we are and how we think, but we have also let negative and underserving people take root in our lives. We allowed that negativity to make us distrustful of others and make us cynical towards relationships, but we refuse to take action simply because we don't want to hurt anyone's feelings. There is no easy way around it however; some people just don't need to move forward with us.

Love Me Right or Not At All

It isn't that we are better than anyone else, but we have to come to a point in our maturing where we understand that some people don't mean us well and just don't need to be in our lives anymore. That is not to say that people can't change, but you're on a journey to become a healthy you. All these steps require you to take action. We have to strive to be honest with ourselves, honest with the people who are in our lives, and honest about the things that hurt us and keep us down. We have spent too much time living in untruths; spent too much time burying hurt, guilt, and shame; mistreating people to hide our own pain, being disrespected by others because we don't want to be alone, and staying in disastrous relationships because we don't love ourselves enough to let go of the things that are destroying us.

STARTING POINT 2: LOVE YOURSELF NOW

Romance Yourself

Loving yourself is not always easy. We struggle with loving ourselves because we don't believe we are deserving of love. This type of thinking has caused us to continue putting ourselves down, allowing others to put us down, and keeping negativity in our lives. Love yourself now, again cannot be a passive action, instead we have to take assertive steps to love who we are, build ourselves up, and be mindful of the type of people we let into our lives. How can we start to love ourselves? We have already worked on changing our mindsets, pressing our reset buttons, rethinking, reviving and resurfacing our hopes and dreams. We have started to look forward, and we know to only look back when we are trying to avoid repeating the past. We also took a brief look at removing past people from our present lives. So now that we have done all the work, or at least have started the active process of doing the work needed, it is time to have a little fun. We can have fun loving who we are by romancing ourselves.

Romance as a verb is defined by Merriam-Webster as, "giving special attention to (someone) in order to get something that you want from that person; to exaggerate or invent detail or incident," (2015). Under normal circumstances we work to romance others and when we romance the ones we love, we often feel good about ourselves, we feel good that we made our loved ones feel good, and there are often rewards that come from romancing others. We can apply this same attitude to ourselves by romancing who we are. This is not falling back into our old ways of thinking and getting too full of ourselves. Instead we are working towards taking some time and paying attention to what makes us feel good, what encourages us, what empowers us, and what makes us want to embrace who we are. The work that has to be done to become a healthier you is not an easy task and the work to stay a healthy you won't be easy. So when we are doing all this hard work we can often get discouraged or unmotivated to continue moving forward and that is why you need a reminder or a grand gesture to help you continue on the path of loving yourself right now; placing yourself on the path to romancing yourself. It can be as literal as buying yourself flowers or sending yourself an encouraging card in the mail. It could be sending yourself an encouraging email telling yourself how excited you are with the progress you have been making toward getting over yourself, making healthy choices, and being mindful of the things you let into your life.

    You can also romance yourself by treating yourself to dinner or celebrating with friends who are also on the path to being their best selves. You can romance yourself by celebrating the anniversary of the moment you decided to get over yourself or take off the mask and walk towards a healthier you. You can romance yourself by writing affirmation statements that empower you to strive to be the best you can be. However you decide to romance yourself, just make sure that you are intentional in doing so.

Don't waste time being fearful of appreciating who you are. Truly loving yourself is not an act of arrogance or being conceited; loving yourself the right way is having healthy esteem for who you are, where you are in your life, and the plans you'll make for your future. It is being mindful of who and what is entering your life, and using that same mindfulness of who and what you let leave your life as well. It can be very romantic when you make the decision not to let negativity enter into your personal space, but also that you are aware of not letting any negativity you may have enter the personal space of those around you. You can romance yourself by just being who you are.

It can be very exhausting and wasteful to work so hard at being someone else and no one really cares that much about the pretending you're doing. So why do we spend so much time investing in pretending and end up miserable and unappreciated?

Love Me Right or Not At All

Take this time to really focus on being a healthy you. Work hard at being a free you and don't squander that time being unhealthy. Romancing yourself is loving yourself. So many of us don't take the time to love the person we are. I hope that what you have read has started you on the path to loving and romancing yourself in a healthy way. The work going forward may become challenging because we have started the path of being aware of loving ourselves, but in these next chapters we are going to learn who we should give our love to. Don't forget to take every chance to romance and encourage yourself.

STARTING POINT 3: GIVE LOVE TO THE RIGHT PEOPLE

Identify Who Belongs in Your Life

The previous chapters have focused on you and loving who you are. We took the steps to unmask ourselves, break free from the lies and the un-forgiveness we may have harbored for years towards ourselves and others. These next chapters, however, will focus on breaking free from the bondage of loving the wrong people. I know that sounds crazy because in most religions and peaceful movements we are taught to love everyone. I am not writing this to tell you not to love people. Love is a powerful force that we all should exercise to as many people as we can. However, these chapters will help us gain an awareness of who we are loving, or rather the energy, time, and actions we are giving, who we are giving it to, and why we are giving this love to people. This chapter in particular will deal with helping us identify who we are loving and why.

Love Me Right or Not At All

The idea is to take control of who you choose to love. I want to take this time to let you know that I am talking more so about the love we give to friends and family; I am also talking about romantic/intimate love as well. This doesn't apply to what is called "agape love" or "unconditional love". I believe we are already very "selective" regarding whom we give that type of love to, but we are very careless with whom we give the other types of love to. Remember we want to take control of who we are friends with, who we are intimate or romantic with, and who we give our time and attention to.

Identifying who belongs in your life can be very scary for some of us. For some people it is very difficult to be, think, or even feel like we are alone. So to think about removing people from our lives is almost like removing the very thing that makes us feel alive. We have become so willing to keep all types of people around us, so that we avoid feeling lonely or being alone, that we ignore or no longer can recognize when people are using, abusing, or even destroying us. On the other side of that coin, it has become habitual for us to use, abuse, drain, and even destroy people who are in our lives for our own personal gain or enjoyment.

Taking control of who is in your life and identifying who belongs in your life is not a list so you can start throwing people out and blaming them for being a negative force in your life. No, it is an evaluative moment for you to recognize that you may need to apologize and remove yourself from the lives of people you haven't treated right or may have used. It is vital for us to love others in a healthy way by evaluating how we treat people as well. Sometimes we feel like we are being mistreated and used, but the reality is we are just reaping the residual outcomes of what we have been giving to others and masking it as love. Identifying who belongs in your life starts with you being honest about whether or not you belong in their lives first and foremost.

Evaluation should start from within. If we are holding ourselves to healthy morals and appropriate standards, we can have a clear picture of the standards we should have for others.

Love Me Right or Not At All

This isn't self-righteousness because the healthy you realizes that you have problems and issues just like the next person. Again, this is coming into a place of awareness because <u>relationship blindness becomes habitual for us.</u> We get entangled in being loved and having people around us and we don't see the destruction that we are causing. We think that, because a big explosion hasn't happened, the relationships that we are in are harmless, but destruction doesn't always occur all at once. Think of the years you have spent being in relationships that weren't any good for you. How these relationships have drained you, hurt you, changed your perspective on love; how being in these destructive relationships has slowly drained you or the other person of the light you once had; how you no longer look at yourself the same way; we nest in hatred and distrust because we have dwelled in unhealthy environments with ourselves and with others all for some need that we believe has to be met. That long-term destruction, to me, is worse than the instant detonation that we often look for. We stay in negative friendships, familial relationships, dating, and even marital relationships, completely unaware of the often life-long devastation these types of relationships are causing. Healing can't begin because we remain exposed to the very person or people who inflicted the wounds. We won't allow other people to heal because we continue to inflict wounds that cause lifetime destruction; we don't let go because we need them around or we want them around. We first identify who belongs in our lives by identifying why they are in our lives. We also have to identify why we are in their lives. If all the arrows point to negativity or a selfish motive, those signs are indicators that they don't or you don't need to be in one another's lives anymore.

We can identify who belongs in our lives by taking an active role in unmasking people. The work that has to be done can't be passive. We have to take an assertive role in removing the wrong people from our lives and be in control of who we are loving. We have to stop trying to leave everything up to fate. We fall into the passive role and relinquish our control after we get into relationships. Beforehand, however, we are out there actively making friends, actively dating, surfing the web and social media for relationships, befriending people from all over the world, going to clubs, bringing people to our beds, meeting their families, hanging out with them, but as soon as we feel comfortable or "safe" we take off the suit of action and we leave it all up to fate. Some of us get into relationships and we even say, "OK, I now give it all to God to work out." It doesn't and it shouldn't work this way. It is important to finish the same way you started. If you didn't start a relationship or friendship with someone by leaving it up to God or leaving it up to fate, you definitely shouldn't expect God or fate to finish the work for you.

We have to take an active role in cultivating and maintaining healthy relationships in all areas of our lives. It starts by taking an active role in identifying who needs to be in your life. It starts with unmasking them for who they really are to you and who you really are to them. The way you think, feel, and act toward one another will be an indication of whether or not they need to be in your life. This can only happen if we are looking through truthful lenses. Do I really mean this person any good? Do I truly care about their well-being? Would I genuinely rejoice if they were doing well or would I genuinely rejoice if they hit rock bottom? These are the questions you ask yourself about them and then switch it around and ask them how they truly feel about you.

Also ask if being around the people you say you love or the person you're in love with is an exceptionally positive influence on your life. This influence can't be something that is temporary or fleeting; it can't just be based on fickle feelings that you receive from the person or they receive from you every once in a while. This influence should be positive in all areas of your life. You and the individuals who are sharing love and sharing space truly are about seeing, developing, and enriching the growth that is needed for both individuals moving forward. When you absolutely love someone, you don't spend time in negativity concerning them and you can't sit by and watch destructive things happening to them without some type of intervention on your part or vice versa.

It is difficult for people to hide their true motives for too long if we have set the right atmosphere for the people we love. If we have positive expectations for those around us and we don't tolerate or accept negativity, negative people have a difficult time being around that. Negative people often crave negativity. They function well in it and they grow from it. When there is an absence of negativity, negative people get bored. When they get bored, they either get desperate in creating negativity in the lives of others or they move on to find other people who will feed their desires for negativity. That is why it is important to evaluate yourself and see if you're a negative person and to also see if you allow negative people in your life. If you do, take the time now to change your mindset and environment. I'm not asking you to label yourself as an optimist or pessimist, but we should try to look at ourselves as healthy and realistic people. Realistic enough to first understand that you don't have it all together and neither does anyone else. Realistic enough to set appropriate boundaries with others and to set up rules for people you allow in your life.

We have to take an active role in what we let into our lives and who we allow in our personal environments. We have been too careless with whom we give our love to all for the sake of not feeling lonely. Some of us know that it is time to unmask people if we say, "<u>It is better to be miserable than to be alone</u>." If you believe this statement, it is a clear sign that some healing and assertive action needs to take place. We can't be afraid to let go of people who don't belong. We have to be willing to remove the masks that we have placed on people for our own means.

We have forcefully transformed the wrong people into our "queens" or "knights in shining armor" because of unmet needs or dreams that we have that have not been realized. We fall in love with the wrong people because we envy what our friends and family have and we become inpatient with the process. We

Love Me Right or Not At All

work hard to make people into what we want them to be despite them showing who they are. We refuse to believe this person or groups of people can't be wrong for us and so we create masks for them and we make them look good. We make them out to be what we desire them to be and ignore who is truly in front of us. We can see that they are covered in wounds old and new, but we actively participate in picking the scabs and adding fresh poison to an already infected wound. Then, after we have already become enmeshed in each other's hurt and pain until we can't tell where their hurt begins and ours ends, we say, "There is no escape," and "I don't know how we got here." We can only unmask people when we are willing to stop putting masks on them in the first place. Once we unmask them, we can see clearly whether or not this is the right person to give love, time, and attention to.

Another way to identify whether or not people belong in your life is to consider what they say about you when you're not around. Let me point out that there is no way for you to control how people think, act, or feel; you can, however, in some instances, shape what they say about you based on the way you treat them. If you have people around you who you treat well and you don't talk bad about them, those individuals should, in turn, do right by you as well. People enjoy talking about and praising the people they love. So if you're doing right by others, it shouldn't come as a surprise when others come to you and say, "You know your friends speak very highly of you. I can see what they see in you."

In some cases, however, there are some people you treat well, you love on them and you speak nothing but their praises, but every now and then you hear or see that they don't have positive things to say about you. These are the people who need to be unmasked and removed from your life. I'm not talking about if they go and say something that is true about you based on something you may have done wrong or even when you make a mistake. We spend too much time trying to avoid being corrected or avoid accepting that we have wronged someone;

Love Me Right or Not At All

rather we defend our poor choices or unacceptable actions just to avoid repenting. So that's not what I am referring to here. We want to look at when we know that we have done right by others in word, thought, and deed but they still feel the need to speak negatively about us, spread untruths about us, or create negativity. These are the individuals that you need to let go of. Notice that I didn't say you stop loving them, but you have to stop allowing them to have your time, energy, and feelings. You can identify them based on how they respond when you confront them about what they have said. If they respond like they never said it, or they aggressively try to defend themselves, or they try to shift the blame to others, they are not the ones you should give your time, energy, and feelings to.

We have to identify people by what they say about us when we aren't around, but we also have to identify how we respond to what has been said. We have to work really hard not to get upset or out of control when we hear what someone has said about us behind our backs. It is important to recognize that they said it behind our backs and not to us. This is an indication that what was said was only meant to try to destroy us, but ultimately make us get in our feelings. It is also important to recognize that we often get mad at the negative things people say, not because they are factual or truthful, but because, on some level, we believe those things about ourselves. We have to do the work to build ourselves up and to encourage the people around us to build themselves. Our response to what people say and how people treat us is the determining factor in whether or not we are ready to grow past all the negativity. Remember the only way for negativity to grow is if it is fed negatively. That's why I wanted to make clear that we should not stop loving people, but we do need to be careful who we give love to.

We will talk a little bit more about identifying people, but I want to say that you can truly identify who belongs in your life by their willingness to be there. I want to be clear that everyone can't spend all of their time, energy, and feelings on you; you can't spend all your time, energy, and feelings on them either.

Love Me Right or Not At All

The key is when you do show love to the right people and when they show love to you that it is done with quality. We think quantity is the answer, but the reality is there are a lot of people giving you a whole lot of destructive time, actions, and feelings in great quantities; we count them as friends and loved ones because of how much we see of them and they don't make us feel lonely, but how much of what they are doing is actually worth anything positive? How much of what they do for you is actually healthy? Some of the healthiest and strongest relationships are the ones in which people may not spend countless amount of time with one another, but when they come together the quality of that time spent is priceless and beneficial.

You'll know you're giving love to the right people when it generates growth in some or all areas of your life in some way. You'll know you are giving love to the right people when your love helps them grow as well. We should seek relationships that are beneficial. Not for superficial gain, but it is beneficial to making you and them better people. Stop only focusing on the quantity, but assess whether or not the relationship has quality. You will know that you are giving love to the right people when you can identify whether the relationship, the love, and the actions have quality. If someone wants to add quality to your life they will do just that. They will desire to spend time with you and ensure that each time you do get to spend time together you are growing. Individuals, groups, and families who are trying to cultivate relationships with others have to be intentional in confirming that growth will take place when they encounter one another.

Growth of that caliber can only happen when love, time, attention, and feelings are operating from a healthy place and it is given to the right people. When we become drained of our resources—time, energy, feelings, and love—we become distrustful and cynical. When that happens we miss out on the opportunities to build healthy and powerful relationships with the right people because we no longer have good ground to grow with and we no longer have anything positive to deposit in the

Love Me Right or Not At All

lives of others. What isn't growing or can gain access to growth ends up dying. When the potential for growth is smothered by the wrong people, our potential becomes a graveyard and it is home to zombie-like creatures who only seek to drag other people down with them. We have to identify how we think, feel, and act towards other people, assess how people think, feel, and act towards us, and identify who we need to let go of or if they need to let go of us. This isn't to hurt feelings or to isolate you from the world; on the contrary, this step is for you to identify who belongs in your life and who will have a positive impact on your life in some way. Take off the masks and truly identify who belongs in your life.

STARTING POINT 3: GIVE LOVE TO THE RIGHT PEOPLE

Identify Who Doesn't Belong and Ask Them to Leave

"We have to learn how to give some people the gift of goodbye!" My Bishop, Lanier C. Twyman of the St. Stephen Baptist Church, said the quote above and it was one of the most profound statements I have ever heard. It has helped shape the basis for this chapter. We have to identify who doesn't belong in our lives and ask them to leave. In many instances we have relinquished control of our thoughts, feelings, actions, and decisions over to people who have not had our best interests at heart. In other instances we have taken control or tried to control those same areas in the lives of others; a never-ending cycle of controlling and hurting people that ultimately destroys. We have to take control of our lives and be mindful and aware of the people that are in our lives, mindful of how each and every

Love Me Right or Not At All

person we interact with shapes how we think, feel, and behave. If we have people in our lives who help us grow, they support us and they love us with no strings attached; we should nurture, appreciate, and cultivate those relationships. We should also invest in those positive relationships and ensure that we are helping others grow, they feel supported by us, and we love them with no strings attached. However, if we identify that the people in our lives do nothing but drain us, take from us, and put us down, we need to take an active and assertive role in asking them to leave. There are just some people who don't belong in our lives and we have to be OK with saying goodbye to them. I like that we can look at it from a positive aspect and present it as a gift.

Saying goodbye to someone you have been friends with or been in a relationship with for a long time can be very difficult. This difficulty can lead us to believe that we have to keep them in our lives or stay in their lives so no one will be hurt; we often try to avoid feeling like we have failed because we have decided to throw in the towel. It can be a challenging process if we continue to try to hold on to something that is dead. It is understandable to try to save something that is dying, but when you know that a relationship is dead and neither party wants to be resuscitated, holding on can be detrimental to everyone involved. By asking them to leave you could possibly be giving everyone a gift—the gift of starting over, the gift of changing, and the gift of moving forward.

Getting caught up in feeling like longevity is the only indicator for relationship stability can cause us to stay in unhealthy relationships and continue to be around people we know don't mean us well. Identifying who belongs helps us to take control over who is in our lives and asking them to leave empowers us to be in control of who goes and who stays.

Oftentimes we struggle with asking people to leave because we believe that we can change them and make everything better. Change in a person or a person changing is an internal decision and transformation that has to be voluntarily accepted within

Love Me Right or Not At All

that person. People can change based on their situations or environments, but the key word is "can" change. That means that it is based on them deciding to change. We can't change anyone and no one can change us. You are fighting a losing battle and setting yourself up for failure when you set out to try to change the ones you love or the ones you're in relationship with. You can communicate your thoughts and feelings concerning the need for change in their lives, but no matter how hard you try, how many ultimatums you dish out, and how many times you threaten to leave, that person must choose to change or choose to stay the same. We can't delay asking negative people to leave or letting go of toxic relationships because we believe that we can change them. We only have the power to change within ourselves and we have to leave the responsibility of our loved ones changing to them.

It can be very difficult to say goodbye to people we truly love and care about, but once you have evaluated the relationship and you see that the relationship/friendship is deadly—you may have even tried to fix things, but nothing has improved—you have to take an assertive role and either ask them to leave or say goodbye to them.

We also have to stop trying to make people stay if they want to leave. Just as we can't make them change, we can't try to force them to stay. Sometimes we spend too much time trying to make something that is clearly not working work; we do this because we struggle with loneliness, being alone, fear, and a host of other issues that make us believe that we have to stay in destructive relationships. When we find the courage to let go or the strength to walk away, we may discover all the things that were missing within ourselves and also see a clearly painted picture of what to avoid in our next relationship.

STARTING POINT 3: GIVE LOVE TO THE RIGHT PEOPLE

You Will Need to Rinse and Repeat

We are learning to give love to the right people by identifying who belongs in our lives. We aren't saying we are better than anyone else, but we are taking control over what is being poured into our lives and what needs to be drained from our lives. We also work to identify whether we ourselves belong in the lives of the people we interact with and are in relationship with. We acknowledge that, sometimes and in certain situations, we may be toxic to people and we take responsibility for exiting their lives. None of this is easy and it won't be easy to disrupt the way we have been living for quite some time. The people we interact with, hang out with, and the individuals we are in relationships with are really fun to be around, meet our needs, and help us feel wanted. This process of letting go can be scary and challenging, but we are looking to love people the right way; working to love ourselves in a healthy way. That type of love is going to take some hard work, but when we embrace this process we begin to recognize that, although they did fulfill some needs, the relationship itself isn't any good for any of the parties involved, and it what could be best for all of us is to say goodbye.

Although we find ourselves identifying the people who can stay and the people we may have to say goodbye too, oftentimes we get caught up in the feelings of, "This is too hard," or "I want to give them another chance." To be honest, there isn't anything wrong with giving people another chance—giving them another chance after we have clearly communicated what is healthy, what is unhealthy; identified what is acceptable and what is unacceptable in the relationship; clearly identified what is positive and what is negative. Giving another chance isn't a bad thing, but we also have to accept that, if we let them back in, we may need to rinse and repeat the process of identifying who belongs in our lives, identifying who doesn't belong, and taking a stance by asking them to leave.

When it comes to changing, we sometimes expect the process to be quick and simple, but frequently the process is long and challenging. We find ourselves giving up on the process and accepting the relationships for what they are. We end up repeating the mistakes of our past and repeatedly allowing dangerous people into our lives, our hearts, and our minds. This is why we have to "rinse and repeat" the process of letting go, identifying who we should keep in our lives because they help us grow, tell us the truth, support us, and build us. We also have to rinse and repeat the process of identifying who doesn't belong in our lives and asking them to leave; not because we are mean or we are conceited, but we recognize that we can't reach our healthy selves if we are influenced by unhealthy people.

We rinse to eliminate all of the debris and fallout that will come from the process of purging. We rinse so that we can see

Love Me Right or Not At All

what it looks like to have once had all the negativity and destruction in our lives, but to also watch it go down the proverbial or imaginary drain, and out of our lives. While evaluation can be a very helpful and insightful process, it can also be very overwhelming to pick apart your relationships; to see how well you treat people in relationships and assess how well they treat you; to exam if you are actually a positive force in someone's life, and for you to dissect whether or not they add value to your life. This can be a monumental task, but necessary for trying to become a healthy individual and helping those around you become healthy individuals. We can't go from unhealthy to healthy without going through a process; and no process is worth going through if there isn't some form of challenge that comes with it. It is going to take some work to get through identifying who should stay and who should go when it comes to your relationships. You may miss or even overlook some people because of how long you've known them, what they do for you, and what they mean to you. Let's be clear; not

Love Me Right or Not At All

everyone will need to leave and some positive results will come from you identifying who belongs and who doesn't belong in your life. Rinsing and repeating will give you the opportunity to check in when needed or take the time to ensure that you have made all the right choices on who you are giving love to. We want to give love to people who want to be loved and they want to give love right back.

STARTING POINT 3: GIVE LOVE TO THE RIGHT PEOPLE

Manage Love the Right Way with the Right People

Relationships on all levels take work. There is no way to properly and responsibly manage a relationship with someone if you don't put in the time and effort needed to maintain a strong and healthy relationship. We lose out on rewarding and healthy relationships because we become too comfortable and neglectful of our relationships; we often forget to be present in the lives of the ones we say we love. It is important that we learn how to manage the love we have for one another the right way. We have already taken the steps to identify who belongs in our lives and who doesn't, so now we should have a good idea of the people we have decided to be in relationship with. We have the "right people" or the people that will help us grow, be honest with us, have fun with us, and motivate us to reach our best selves. Why wouldn't we want to manage these relationships the right way? It is unhealthy for us to be afraid or too lazy to put in the work necessary to maintaining and managing a healthy friendship, family relationship, romantic/intimate relationship, and a maintaining a healthy marriage. If we truly seek to give love to the right people, we have to embrace that it is going to take some hard work and dedication to ensure that we are mutually bringing positive vibes, genuine love, care, concern, hope, peace, and fun to the relationships we have identified as healthy and positive to us becoming our best selves.

We have taken off the mask of untruthfulness and we are no longer placing the blame on others for the mistakes and troubles that are in our lives. Now that we have taken full accountability for our choices and actions we can take full advantage of the freedom and free will that we have to manage love the right way with the right people. The healthy way to do this is through first accepting that we are making the choice to have the right people in our lives and accepting those individuals for who they are.

We are not trying to change anyone, but we are focusing on loving who we are so that we can effectively love the people we are friends with, the people we are family with, and even the person we choose to be in an intimate relationship with. Managing this love in a healthy way can only work if we are no longer engaging our relationships in autopilot mode. We have to be present and accounted for in our friendships and relationships if we and the people we are in relationship with want to get the most out of the relationships.

We can't manage love the right way and with the right people if we don't love ourselves. It is our responsibility to love who we are. If we are unhappy with ourselves and with our lives, we will spend the most time making others pay for our unhappiness. We have to pay attention to not only the truth in what our friends say about us when we aren't around, but also the message they are telling us right to our faces. What they are saying is often a clear indicator of how we treat them and what they truly feel about us; how we treat the ones we like and love

Love Me Right or Not At All

is often a clear indicator of how we feel about ourselves. It is unhealthy to run around trying to manage relationships with others when we are incapable of managing how we feel about ourselves. We are miserable and disappointed with ourselves for a number of reasons, we don't deal with it, we blame others for what is happening in our lives, and we treat those who are close to us like they are our punching bags or therapist. We put too much weight on our friends, loved ones, and spouses to "fix" us, but we don't want the help that they offer. If we are loving the right people, the right people won't let us go on a self-destructive path or allow us to be destructive in their lives.

You thought that giving love to the right people was for you only? No, loving the right people is also for the people who love you. They are accountable for being truthful and encouraging to you, just as you should be to them. They won't allow you to hold them back from being great, just as you shouldn't allow them to hold you back. There is a healthy level of give and take in these healthy and well-managed relationships because all

Love Me Right or Not At All

parties involved should have the understanding that loving yourself is vital first and foremost, but also understanding that being "fake", insincere, unapologetic, unmotivated, not present, unrealistic, and uncompromising isn't healthy for a relationship or the people involved. Giving love to the right people isn't about controlling people and neither is managing that love; giving love to the right people is more about taking control of what is allowed into the relationship and what will be removed out of the relationship because everyone involved recognizes that those things will cause destruction.

We can't keep projecting our pain, disappointment, and sadness onto our friends and significant others because they allow us to. We have to manage those feelings and emotions; we have to reconcile them, put them in their proper place, and reach a place of healing. The friends and loved ones we have chosen to love and give love to shouldn't be the dumping grounds for our emotional waste, instead they should be the bridge or ladder builders to help us reach greater heights, reach our potential, and to be there at the top with us to celebrate our success.

Managing this type of love will be difficult if we don't do the work needed to identify who truly belongs in our lives and if we truly belong in theirs; it won't work if we don't ask the people who don't belong to leave. There shouldn't be any room left for us to continue to treat the people we love like they owe us or that they deserve to be treated in a disrespectful manner. This also applies to how people treat us. It is not OK to say we love one another but not display that love in our actions. If we love the right people and the right people love us, we won't have to worry about being talked about behind our backs in a negative way, we won't have to worry if their intentions are genuine, and we won't have to be concerned about whether they will be supportive of us.

Taking an active role in who you love and taking care to manage that love is very important in maintaining a healthy you. The people that we are in relationship with truly contribute to how we view ourselves and how we behave. You can't expect to grow and be successful if you continue to surround yourself with people who are comfortable in failure and conformity. Surround yourself with people who have goals, who are accountable to overcoming their limitations, and set out to achieve greatness. Make up your mind to be around positive people! Managing this type of love the right way isn't easy, but if you're intentional and serious about being a healthier person you will take the steps to manage the right kind of love.

We manage love the right way by being available to those we love and the right people love us and they are available to us. Availability is very important in a healthy relationship. It lets the people you love know that you are serious about them and that you love them enough to give them something you can't ever get back and that is time. I have heard it said that time is a precious commodity and so what is a better indicator that you love someone one than giving them your time? Managing love the right way and with the right people involves your availability to the relationship. No one wants to be friends with or in an intimate relationship with someone who is unavailable. They can't ever reach you to hang out, they can't depend on you in a crisis, and you're not there during significant moments in their lives. Being unavailable will cause people to write you off or put you on the backburner. You may have a friend or a partner who can forgive your unavailability and genuinely show up for you, but underneath the surface they may feel very disconnected from you and possibly even resentful of you. That is why it is important to choose the right people to love so that you can effectively manage that love. You will invest in the relationships that matter most to you, but you will also work hard for the people you know will do the same for you.

It is not easy to make these choices, but fear and loneliness can no longer be the deciding factors in who you decide to be friends with. Fear and the thought of being alone can't be the motivation for you to have friendships or be in intimate relationships. These are unhealthy motivators to building and managing relationships. When we build our relationships based on fear, we tend to only make ourselves available to those relationships in order to get our needs met. Once our needs are met in the relationship or we get our love "fix", we tend to become neglectful of the time spent with our friends and loved ones. When we love others the healthy way, we make time for them, we make quality time for them, and if we are managing love the right way with the right people they make quality time for us as well. It is impossible to have a healthy relationship with others if no one is available.

This availability extends deeper than just quality time, it also looks at whether we are emotionally and mentally available as well. Many of our relationships are unhealthy because we have not accepted that we entered into these relationships mentally and emotionally unavailable. We can't give to others or be present for others because there are unresolved issues underneath the surface fighting to get into our space of awareness. We continue to bury them under the disguise of

Love Me Right or Not At All

having a lot of friends, being in a series of intimate relationships, or putting our entire focus on our career goals. While having friends, having intimate relationships, and focusing on your career aren't bad things, having these things while you are emotionally and mentally unavailable will cause these areas in your life to become unmanageable; they become unmanageable to the point that you lose them and they no longer serve the purpose of burying the unresolved issues. Now you are faced with the loss of your relationships and your career objectives, you also have to face the unearthed issues you have ignored, and you have to possibly face them alone. The identified goal here is to acknowledge whether or not we are mentally and emotionally available to manage a relationship in a healthy way.

We can't effectively manage love the right way if we are making people pay for the past mistakes of others. We can't successfully be a listening ear for our friends and family if we are often drifting off into our own problems. We can't navigate the intricate dynamics of building a healthy relationship with others if we are not in touch with what we need to resolve internally. Self-care, emotionally and mentally, is very important in trying to establish a healthy life and a healthy mindset. We can't hold the people we love emotionally hostage because we are closed off and unfocused. We can't expect our loved ones to free us from our internal struggles and limitations; they can walk with us towards healing, but they can't heal our problems and we have to stop expecting people to fix us. Managing love with the right people can only happen if we are or we are working towards becoming emotionally and mentally available. We say to ourselves that we want to be available in order for the ones we love to know how much our friendship or relationship means to us.

    Again, managing love the right way with the right people isn't about control or control over others. Instead it is empowering your freedom of choice but also strengthening your ability to give your best to the relationship while receiving the best from the people you are in a relationship with. We manage

Love Me Right or Not At All

love the right way because it is the right thing to do. We have made the decision to be better people and we have activated our power to choose; we choose to be around positive and empowering people. We come together as friends, family, or significant others to reach greatness and positivity. We understand that our friends and loved ones are not dumping grounds and punching bags, but they are our support and our strength; we understand that we should be a strong support for them as well. We have come into some sort of awareness that we can't abuse our relationships simply because we know the people will forgive us and stay around, but we acknowledge our shortcomings and we will make the effort to admit when we are wrong and ask to be forgiven. This is what it means to manage love the right way with the right people.

STARTING POINT 4: LOVE WITH BALANCE

Keep Your Word and Be Honest

We have now moved into the next starting point that directs us to Love with Balance. Balance is defined by the Merriam-Webster dictionary as follows: "…to equal or equalize in weight, number or proportion; to make steady by making weight equal on all sides." Balance, as defined within loving people the healthy way, is to take the lessons from the first three starting points and apply them equally inwardly and towards the people you are in relationship with. You also apply that balance to starting point five and enjoy loving others, but do it in a balanced way so that you are aware of what is happening in your relationships. To Love with balance is going to take practice. It is going to take us first being aware of who we are, what our experiences have taught us, and who we are in relationship with.

Love Me Right or Not At All

As several of the previous chapters have explained, it all starts with us.

We are often unbalanced in our relationships because we start with the other person, we focus on what the other person is doing, and we become fully enmeshed or entangled in the other person's life rather than being fully aware of ourselves. This unbalanced way of loving often causes us to be unfocused on what changes we need to make, how our hurts affect us or hinder us; unaware of the damage our behaviors and words are causing in the relationship, nonchalant about other's thoughts and feelings; focused only on how the person should make us feel and what we are doing to chase after that feeling. That is why we have to love with balance and start by being fully engaged in what is going on with us first. Balancing a love for ourselves first is something that we struggle with, oftentimes because society, television, and even literature teach us to love others and seek the love and approval of others first and foremost. It can be a very selfless thing to love someone else first and give them all your love, but it often becomes unbalanced and very selfish because we are only loving them so that we can receive the love and attention we crave from them. It is a healthy start when we can love ourselves first and balance the love we have for others. It is a challenging, yet rewarding, feat when we can evaluate ourselves, become aware of our strengths and limitations, and set goals for ourselves with love and respect so that we can reciprocate those same feelings towards the people we love and care about. There are several ways that we can love with balance, but in these next few chapters we are going to explore how to love with balance. The first way to Love with Balance is to Keep Your Word and Be Honest.

We often struggle with keeping our word and doing exactly what we say we are going to do. This is one of the biggest barriers in trying to build successful, strong, and healthy relationships on all levels. It is often said that your word is all you have and often the only thing that you can stand on. Even the Bible discusses the power that lies in the words that we utter.

Love Me Right or Not At All

People trust what we say way before they trust what we do. So it is very important that we are mindful of what we say to people in our relationships and that we balance our words with our actions. To put it another way, we need to do exactly what we say we are going to do. The hardest thing to gain is someone's trust, but it is exceedingly easy to break the trust of those we love. We often lose the trust of those we love when we don't keep our word. It is far easier to be honest about what you can do and what you can't do; to be honest about what we are willing to change and what we are unwilling to change; to say what we expect and what we won't accept from the relationship.

The words that we speak are often linked to what we think and feel. Those thoughts and feelings are tied into how we behave. We have to let our words line up with our actions. It is not an easy thing to break down walls and expose vulnerabilities in order to trust someone. So when someone does that for us, when someone trusts us and lets us in, we have to appreciate that and embrace it. We can appreciate them trusting us and being vulnerable towards us by being honest with them and keeping our word. Have you ever been in a relationship or a friendship with someone and you were completely open and vulnerable with them but they were closed off and guarded? How did it make you feel? Did that unbalanced dynamic affect you in any way? This is not a great feeling, especially when you are trying your very best to be open, honest, and vulnerable with them. This eventually leads to you feeling hurt, that hurt turns into resentment, and that resentment turns into inward anger, and eventually that anger is directed towards them causing what could be a disaster. If you are familiar with this scenario, imagine if the scenario happens because you have not been very trustworthy and forthcoming. It takes a lifetime to build trust, but a moment to break it when we don't keep our word or remain honest with the ones we love.

    Honesty is not only an incredible tool, it is also a positive place of being and awareness. It is difficult for us to be honest with ourselves and so we often struggle with being honest with others. Honesty is not just telling someone how you truly feel, it is how we live, think, and behave. It is also the ability to know what not to say or what not to do. Being honest is about maturity, recognizing that we can't spend the rest of our lives telling "little white lies" to save ourselves. A great perspective on honesty is this: if we let our yes be yes and our no be no, no one can question who we are or our integrity. That is why keeping your word and honesty go hand and hand. Don't say you'll do something and then neglect to do it. We have to be upfront about our strengths and limitations, our successes and our failures, our triumphs and our struggles; letting this level of honesty and openness go out before us will prevent people from perceiving us wrongly or taking things the wrong way.

This level of honesty must start within us. As with most of the chapters in this book, we have to start with us. We are often taught to be honest with others and then later on in life we have to learn to be honest with ourselves. We are faced with being honest with ourselves after several mistakes or dishonest moments. These things could have possibly been avoided if we spent more time being honest with ourselves first, being honest about our wants and desires, and being honest with our shortcomings and limitations. There is a high price placed on others being honest with us, but we don't put that same cost on us to be honest with others and with ourselves. A lot of times it is frightening to really take an honest look at whom we are, what we want in relationships, and what we want out of life. It is equally frightening to be honest about our flaws, our weaknesses, and our struggles. We only want to expose those things when we are in trouble or we are backed into a corner. However, before starting any level of relationship we need to be honest. We should be honest about who we are, what we expect, what they can expect from us, our strengths, and our limitations. It is a very balanced approach to any relationship when you can keep your word and be honest.

STARTING POINT 4: LOVE WITH BALANCE

Have Realistic Expectations for Them and You

Our expectations most definitely shape the way we treat people and affect the way we receive information from those we call our friends, who we date, who we love, and even who we marry. One of the biggest problems that people face in relationships on all levels is the fact that we have unrealistic expectations of people. It runs even deeper than that because we often have unrealistic expectations for ourselves and, in turn, we have unrealistic expectations for the ones we love. Expectations are both the conscious and unconscious things we tell ourselves we need to see, hear, feel, and think in order for things to either run perfectly or turn into the perfect disaster. We can either be fully aware of our expectations for others or "conscious expectations" and we let ourselves know what we expect from

Love Me Right or Not At All

people, we let our friends know what we expect, and we let our lovers, spouses, and significant others know what we expect. We can also be unaware of our unconscious expectations, but we feel them intensely and we become angry, hurt, or frustrated when these undercover or "unconscious expectations" aren't met.

The conscious expectations seem to be "general", "realistic", and "reasonable"; "I want someone to listen to me," "I want someone who is honest," "Go out on lots of dates and spend quality time with me," "Put me first and put their family first." All of these "expectations" seem pretty reasonable, but we often overlook how we unconsciously expect these things to play out and how that person will interpret those expectations based on how they feel, how they think, what they have experienced, and how they behave.

When what we consciously and unconsciously expect don't line up into how that person interprets our expectations we run into problems. We say we expect people to spend time with us

Love Me Right or Not At All

(consciously), but we really expect them to spend all their time with us (unconsciously + unreasonable). We expect to be forgiven when we wrong someone (conscious expectation), but we really don't want our friends and significant others to ever hold us accountable when we have done wrong (unconscious expectation + unreasonable). They spend an appropriate amount of time paying attention to us (conscious expectation), but we really expect them to only focus on what we like and what we do (unconscious + unreasonable expectation). Another example could be that we expect a person to love all the good about us (conscious expectation + unreasonable), but what we expect that to look like is for them to love us when we are at our worst or all of our flaws (unconscious expectation + unreasonable). We struggle when they are only able to love what we have presented to them but expected them to love every part of us. The point is that we first have to understand what we expect from ourselves when we enter into a friendship or intimate relationship, we then have to communicate and set realistic expectations for the people we are relating with, and finally we have to allow them to communicate what that looks and feels like to them.

Realistic expectations are paramount to any successful relationship. We have to come to the realization that no one person can meet all of our needs or expectations. It does mean that we should recognize that we don't want people to set us up for failure and so we can't set them up for failure as well. You can't go around giving people tests that they have not studied for or even reviewed the material. There are no mind readers or people who can truly empathize with you if you did not communicate with them. There is a need for us to understand and put in check our unrealistic unconscious expectations of people so that we can set and clearly communicate reasonable conscious expectations.

I was talking to my friend Renee, who goes to my church. We were discussing parents having realistic dating expectations for their teenagers. One of the things she said about her daughter was that she understands she will date, have crushes, and want to hang out, but that she wants her to understand that she can't be possessive and claim ownership of any young man. I was blown away by that statement. Many times in life, especially when it comes to relationships, we spend entirely too much energy being overly possessive of a person, addicted to labels (this is my boyfriend, this is my girlfriend, this is my man or my woman), and trying to be in total control of someone else. This translates into very unhealthy ways of thinking and relating to others. It really does start when you're young and not just in teenage dating situations, but even the way children and teenagers view their friendships. This often spills over when you become an adult, especially if you aren't taught the danger of being possessive or claiming ownership of another person.

I remember having this conversation with my friend and thinking about writing this chapter in the middle of our conversation. We walk around in our relationships believing that we are the sun, the moon, and the stars to an individual and that they feel the same way about us. We become consumed with what they are doing day in and day out, how they feel about us, how we feel about them, how much time they spend with us, and how much time they spend with other people. This consumption eventually turns into uncontrolled, raw, and often dangerous emotions that cause strain on our friendships and our relationships; they belong to us, they need to acknowledge me and what we have, and they are making me crazy. Being possessive or overly obsessed with labels is just another form of unrealistic, unreasonable, and unmanaged expectations that, if left unchecked, can lead to serious issues in relationships.

The truth is that we don't own anyone on any level. Whether you're a kid, a teenager, or an adult, no one belongs to you or should be possessed by you. Even if you venture into a long-term companionship or marriage that person is not your possession. It may feel good to label something, but remember the label isn't what makes something positive or powerful or even healthy. Instead, work on getting to know and building a strong bond with the people you are friends with, the people you date, and the person you may eventually marry. When you're loved, you won't want to be possessed or owned; that feeling won't validate you. When you are in a relationship that will last, the labels won't matter because you will be so amazed that you have something that makes the people in it feel loved and appreciated. This conversation I had with my friend wasn't just the inspiration for this chapter, how I'm going to teach my children to make friends and date, it also taught me how not to be possessive of my wife or be overly focused on gender roles in my marriage. It taught me to appreciate what we have and how to embrace what was needed to make our marriage better.

When we become possessive or try to take ownership of a person we begin to overlook their worth as a unique, autonomous, and individualized human being. Instead, the person that we now believe we own becomes an item or what belongs to me. We don't take the time to get to know them or remember why we became so enamored with them in the first place. This allows us to become jealous of the time they spend

Love Me Right or Not At All

with other people, we often become <u>fearful of their personal growth</u>; we fear that if they grow or mature they will leave us, we become very demanding of their time and energy, and it creates an imbalanced dynamic in the relationship or friendship. The goal shouldn't be to take ownership or become possessive of a person, the goals should be to get to know them, for them to help you grow, and for you to assist in their growth. Possession and ownership place the relationship, friendship, or marriage in a box, you and that person are unable to interact fully and with necessary forces outside of the relationship that are needed for growth and maturity. This will either cause resentment in the relationship or this imbalance in the relationship will make it impossible for you or them to walk away from the relationship intact.

Think about what happens to you when you lose a possession that you cared deeply about. You become devastated by the fact that you won't ever be able to replace the item that was once in your possession. Even though you know you can

Love Me Right or Not At All

possibly replace an item that you treasured, it is impossible to replace the sentiment that was invested in that item; it is impossible to replace a person that you have decided you own or possess. That is because everyone is truly unique and, although you might find someone who has some similarities to the last person you placed all your heart and soul into and expected them to do the same, the next person will still have their own set of beliefs, values, feelings, and thoughts. When we take a possessive approach to our relationships we are crushed when those friendships and relationships come to an end. We are so heartbroken that we tend to falsely believe that we will never be able to move on or find anyone else that we will love the same way. However, we jump right into the next relationship and that possessive quality grows and becomes even more dangerous. We feel that devastation greatly and we feel again that we will never find happiness and love. Then we find ourselves in another relationship and turn up that possessiveness to the highest level and that possessive quality could potentially become abuse on many levels and we run into another host of problems. We have to love with balance and truly seek to embrace the beauty of being in relationships with others; that beauty is getting to know them, them getting to know you, and enjoying the time you spend together. It isn't about trying to possess them or control them, but about embracing them and building a strong friendship and companionship. We will get so much more out of treating people with kindness and respect than trying to control them.

It is also important that we be careful of loving people so hard that we feel possessive or unbalanced when that same love isn't reciprocated. People who tend to love hard can be quite amazing. They are always thinking about the people they love, whether they are friends, family, or their partner; they love them with everything they have. This individual knows everyone's birthday and their favorite gifts, they attend all of the events their friends or family throw, and they sacrifice their own happiness sometimes to ensure that the people they love are happy. However, the people that love so hard are often secretly or adversely depressed or unhappy because they don't get the same love and attention from those they love. It sounds incredibly one sided when one person puts everything into the relationship, but they get the bare minimum, people don't show up to the events meant for them, or they don't get back what they put out. Oftentimes these individuals feel slighted, sometimes they are slighted, but more often than not it is because of the unbalanced way they love.

With this intense way of loving people, while it can feel and be incredible for the people you love, the person who is doing the loving is often questioning why they don't receive that type of love back from anyone. These feelings often leave them hurt, depressed, and can lead them to become very unbalanced in the way they view relationships. Again, we are learning how to love with balance. Loving hard isn't a bad thing, but to expect or unconsciously demand that the people we love should love us the same way is unreasonable; it is especially unreasonable if you don't communicate that you want to be loved the same way.

Those of us who love hard have to have an understanding of why we decide to give it all we have to the ones we love. Do we love hard because of something that was missing in our childhood or growing up? Do we love hard because we hope to make the people we love never leave us? Do we love hard because we experienced it before and it was such an incredible feeling that we want to share it with others? Whatever your answer is, it is important to remember that everyone has their own way of loving you or showing you love, you can't be so caught up in loving so hard that you miss how your loved ones are loving on you. Oftentimes the issue isn't that they aren't loving you or showing you love, the problem is that they aren't loving you the way you're loving them. That doesn't sound like a fair exchange for you or the people involved.

The solution could be to balance the way you love and also communicate when you're not feeling very loved by your

Love Me Right or Not At All

friends, family, lover, partner, or spouse. It is OK to add some balance to the way you love. You show up to the important stuff, but you also make sure that you're not always sacrificing your last to make someone else happy at the expense of your own happiness. Do some self-reflection and ensure that your love is coming from the right place, you love hard because it is the right thing to do and you like the way it makes others feel; we don't love hard because we expect it in return or do it to fulfill some insecurity that we have, and we don't do it to make people feel guilty when they fall short of our expectations.

There are those who are on the love-too-hard end of the spectrum and then there are those individuals who struggle with loving others deeply or who struggle with connecting emotionally with others. I want to say that I'm not writing about individuals who are emotionally cut or have some sort of personality disorder that doesn't allow them to feel or have emotional interactions or affect. I'm writing about the individuals who are capable of forming relationships and

Love Me Right or Not At All

friendships but they have difficulties embracing emotions or are challenged by digging deeper into loving someone despite their best effort. This can be frustrating to your friends or significant other who wants to see, hear, and feel that you love them. You want to reciprocate the love and affection that they are showing towards you, but it either feels like too much work, you feel that you can't get it right, or you realize that you're just not into showing the type of emotional connection they are looking for .

There could be several reasons why you struggle with loving others deeply or finding a strong emotional connection. You could have always just been that way, there may have been a lack of love and emotion in your childhood or previous relationships, you could be very guarded against showing that level of connection because you fear that you'll get hurt, or you could have any combination of the things I just mentioned. Sometimes, it could be you're just emotionally lazy and developing and growing to that level of love might just be too much work to do in your eyes. However, you got to the point of

Love Me Right or Not At All

being somewhat emotionally stagnant, if it is affecting the relationships you're in, it may just be time to find some balance. Unlike the person who loves too hard, oftentimes the person who loves just enough to keep the relationship "moving" isn't fazed by whether someone is loving them the same way they love. In most cases, they would embrace it if everyone loved on the same level they did. Still, in most cases, they are often just trying to build up the energy not to be rude or seem ungrateful. As I said, it isn't that they aren't able to love or show love, it just takes a little more work for them to get started. They feel like they are in the relationship, they say, "I love you," when appropriate, and they show up when it is important, but it often doesn't get much deeper than that.

Just as loving too hard can be unbalanced, loving only on the surface can be unbalanced as well. Oftentimes you can have no desire to go deeper in your emotional connection, however this is often very selfish, especially if you haven't communicated your feelings to your significant other, or you have told them you want more but you know that you are unwilling to do the work to make that happen. There is a level of honesty and accountability that has to take place when we are struggling with making that connection. With both extremes there has to be acceptance of who you are and the decision you make to either love hard or love just enough, some personal accountability to self-reflect and communicate your feelings to the ones you love, and to work through whatever issues you may be facing because of your inner motives and drives. I wrote this part of this chapter to bring balance to our relationships. We don't spend enough time getting to know ourselves and our own needs; we spend even less time getting to know the people we befriend or enter into relationships with. The balance of having realistic expectations for yourself and others is a huge step in loving yourself and others the right way. It is OK to cut yourself and others some slack. Put some balance in the way you love and expect things from yourself and others.

STARTING POINT 4: LOVE WITH BALANCE

Admit When You're Wrong and Forgive Others

When we want to love with balance we have to get to a place where we are able to forgive. The honest truth is this: we are all human and human beings will make mistakes and fall short. A part of finding a balance in love is having healthy, realistic expectations; a healthy expectation is that people will fall short and sometimes even hurt you. A lot of times we keep record of the wrong that people do to us and hold grudges. These thoughts and feelings are often poisonous for us and the relationships we are in. They can cause us to be closed off and unbalanced in the way we relate to the people we are connected to. We spend too much energy trying to be mad at people and even more energy trying to stay mad and remember why we were mad with them in the first place. It sounds like too much work to try to hold a grudge against someone and so instead the focus should be on forgiving others. It is not easy to forgive, but it grants so much freedom not to have to be bound by the hurt and anger you have decided to hold against the people who have wronged you. The subtitle of this chapter is "Admit When You're Wrong and Forgive Others." The main theme of this entire book is that you must start with you, building a healthy and loving relationship with yourself first, and then apply the healthy lessons of loving yourself first to loving others. So, if you want to get to a place of being able to forgive and understanding the power of forgiveness, you have to first begin with being humble enough to admit when you're wrong and ask to be forgiven.

It starts with you! We can't possibly begin to fully understand the power of forgiveness if we don't know how to admit when we are wrong and, in turn, say that you are sorry for wronging someone else. It is often very difficult to admit you were wrong or that you have wronged someone, because most times we are too stubborn to believe that we are always right. It can be very detrimental to any form of relationship if we can never say that we were at fault and then say, "I am sorry." We can't expect people to love us, trust us, or open up to us if we are too stubborn and selfish to admit when we have done wrong and to ask them to forgive us. As I said before, it is an incredibly humbling experience to have to first admit you're wrong and then to say you're sorry. However, humility teaches us so many lessons; to be unselfish, to think of others, to gain empathy or sharing in the understanding/emotion of other people, to meet others where they are, to serve others, and it gives us strength. So when you admit when you were wrong you allow others to see that you are human and you make mistakes, but it also shows them that you care enough about how they feel that you would make yourself vulnerable to admit fault and then ask to be forgiven.

You have to be genuine in your pursuit of becoming a healthy you and building healthy relationships and that comes with genuinely being able to say, "I was wrong for what I did and I hope that you can forgive me." We focus so much on being right or being the winner, when the focus should be on treating others the way you want to be treated. How often do you become upset because someone wronged you and they won't acknowledge it? How many times have you held a grudge against someone because they wronged you and tried to breeze through life like they didn't do anything wrong? Imagine the way you feel and then imagine how the people who you refuse to apologize to may feel about you. Think about the feeling you get when someone has wronged you and they apologize to you. Doesn't it make you feel better; especially when the person who is apologizing is someone you love or care deeply about? This is why it is important for you to admit when you're wrong and apologize because it will allow them to see that you care more about them than you care about being right.

If you can admit when you are wrong and work on doing your best not to intentionally wrong people, you can possibly find a way to be more open to forgiving others. It is often said that "forgiveness is not for them, but it is more for you" (the person who is doing the forgiving). I believe, however, that the transaction of asking to be forgiven and doing the forgiving is a full and complete two-way transaction. I believe that, in some way, both people benefit from the process of forgiveness. The process of forgiving—asking for forgiveness, and being forgiven—is such a powerful expression of both humility and strength; a process that is full of diverse emotions that eventually lead to freedom and weights being lifted. When we hold grudges we are often powerless to the emotional and mental strain that is upon us when the people or person we are angry with or hurt by comes around us. We are led to believe that by holding a grudge against them we are retaining control over that person and controlling the ability for them not to hurt us anymore. It is often that we find ourselves not in control of anything, even our own emotions, and we are adversely affected by remaining angry rather than being freed because we are in control. We can honestly only be in control of our thoughts, actions, and feelings towards others and not the other way around. There is no way to truly stop people from hurting us. However, we have power over how we respond and whether or not we will forgive them.

The ability to forgive is not a weakness, but a strength. The process leading up to us forgiving someone could teach us why what they did hurt us, whether we had the right response, what forgiving them will do for us, and ultimately how much freedom we will obtain when we forgive them. For a long time I was a grudge holder and I was excellent at holding a grudge and staying angry with people. It often left me emotionally exhausted and mentally unstable because I had to put so much energy into staying mad, remembering why I was mad, and making sure I thought of ways to make them pay. Over the years that anger only poisoned me physically, mentally, and emotionally; the people who were the target of my anger and grudge moved on with their lives and it didn't affect them at all how mad I was at them or even how hurt I was by what they did to me. Not in all cases but most cases, when I went to them and explained how they hurt me and how it affected me, I got their attention, and when I forgave them there was a welcomed response that resonated from them. Notice that I said "in most cases" they responded very positively to me saying that I forgave them; in other cases it didn't faze them in any way at all. Sometimes the response was as if I should apologize for wasting their time. This, however, didn't bother me because I freed myself. I freed myself from being hurt or angry with them and I was able to walk away with that freedom and control that I had lost from years of being angry with someone who didn't care anyway.

If we are going to love with balance we have to learn how to forgive others. Forgiving others is a balanced way of showing your love for other people, but also a balanced way to keep you aware and in control of your own mental and emotional capabilities. Forgiving others is a part of loving others just as much as saying, "I love you," or giving them flowers. It isn't always easy to forgive, but when you start forgiving and you truly believe in the benefits that you receive from forgiving people, it will become a process that you won't mind working towards for building and maintaining a healthy you.

STARTING POINT 4: LOVE WITH BALANCE

Be Loyal, Show Affection, and Give Space When Needed

Loyalty is a powerful tool in all types of relationships that I believe has become overlooked and undervalued. In this new age, having people on the side (male or female) has become very commonplace, and being loyal to all of those different people is overwhelmingly ignored. Literally, if the side-chick or the side-dude isn't playing their "role" or behaving, you can easily replace them with someone else. In many of these unbalanced relationships the belief is that you are being loyal to your main chick or main dude if you don't leave them because they aren't acting right, but you keep them on and just add someone on the side to meet the need that the main person isn't fulfilling. This isn't loyalty in my opinion. In many instances it is a way to avoid dealing with tough situations within the relationship.

Love Me Right or Not At All

The argument isn't that I want everyone to equate loyalty to monogamous relationships. I fully believe in monogamy, but my point in this chapter is the idea of embracing the power and the principle of being loyal to your friends, loyal to your relationships, and loyal to yourself. Loyalty is about being trustworthy, faithful, and devoted. To be loyal is to be consistently intentional to maintaining the trust people have in you and being accountable to those people. In an intimate relationship, if you and your significant other agree that you both are in a committed one-on-one relationship, you should be loyal to that agreement. If at any time you feel you no longer possess the ability or desire to remain loyal to the relationship, you should have a discussion with your significant other that you want to move on or come up with another arrangement that will work for the both of you, so that you both can remain in a relationship.

We can't try to avoid being loyal by being manipulative and calling it loyalty. The biggest test of loyalty is that people can

Love Me Right or Not At All

count on you to do what you say you'll do and own up to the things you're unable to do; it is the same test that you give to the people you're in relationship with. Can I trust you in this relationship? Will you be honest with me if the rules of the relationship no longer work for you? Can you walk away from the relationship and be honest about why you're walking away without trying to create a black hole full of drama and hurt just to avoid the difficulty that comes from a break up or ending an arrangement? I think cheating or making it known that you will have someone on the side are the easy and often detrimental ways to avoid healthy conflict and conflict resolution. Cheating, infidelity, adultery, and side-pieces are all ways that I believe some people use to either give them an "excuse" to walk away from the relationship, create new dynamics or rules for the relationship, or to avoid the tough conversations that are needed when the relationship has reached a crossroad. Whatever the case may be, I think that we have to be open and honest about what we want in a relationship; to avoid tainting the idea of loyalty because we are too afraid of being honest with ourselves and with the people we are in relationship with about what we want and what we want to do.

My father always used to say, "In relationships, son, you want someone who can be honest enough with you about what they want and what they expect out of the relationship. Basically, you want someone who will always give you an option or a choice. You don't want to be with someone who will make the decision for you. You can't make the choice for anyone else either. You are either going to be loyal to that one person or you're going to be loyal to the fact that you want to be with more than one person and be honest with every single person regarding what you are about. Don't go around expecting people to love a cheater who is pretending to be monogamous. Don't go around making choices for people or letting people make choices for you."

I used to ask my father all the time why he thought people cheated or why people couldn't remain loyal in relationships. He

Love Me Right or Not At All

would often say that they were selfish or too afraid to be loyal. We know that there are a million excuses that someone could give for not being loyal, but my father is not a man of many excuses. With my father, it is either you do or you don't. You are either going to be loyal or you'll be disloyal. The idea of cheating is often very foreign to people who pride themselves on being loyal. Loyalty runs much deeper than just "not cheating", it also speaks to keeping your word, being dependable, responsible for others, accountable to others, and building trust within others. Loving with balance includes loyalty; being real and truthful with those you are in a friendship, family-ship, relationship, partnership, or marriage with. You are able to be trusted and counted on when needed. You can't expect someone to be loyal who never had that expectation within themselves. Loyalty is a choice, but it's also a quality that we possess within ourselves. We walk in imbalance when we get into relationships with someone we know is incapable of being loyal. We walk in imbalance when we enter into relationships knowing that loyalty isn't something we can commit to. We can't begin to be consistent to who we say we are and do exactly what we say we will do if we are lying to ourselves.

What most people present on the outside or what they say is often a mask or a filtered version of what they are really thinking or feeling. It is not a common occurrence for someone to be completely honest about who they are, what they are truly feeling, and what they actually believe about themselves. Those thoughts and feelings are often locked tightly within themselves and most times they can't even fully access what they are truly feeling. Loyalty or the conviction to be loyal is assumed, but it is never truly discussed. It has been my experience that you have to have that conversation in relationships so that you can see where a person is coming from. This process is going to take some time. I know that for modern day relationships everything has to be done quickly, but to truly understand someone's convictions, to find out what they truly want and desire, you have to take the time to have a conversation with them. In order to attempt to gain some insight into whether or not a person can be loyal and committed, to see if someone can be trustworthy, it is going to take an intimate conversation.

If you didn't start with chapter one, I want you to go back and read about taking off the mask. On some level, I believe we all wear a mask that is meant to protect us or propel us, but in actuality it hides us and holds us back. To find balance we have to talk about what we truly want out of a relationship and what we expect from ourselves, what we expect from the people we are in relationship with, and what we are willing to be loyal to. Can I be loyal to you when you change? That is often the hardest part of being in a committed relationship or friendship. We struggle so much with loving someone when they change, even if they change for the good of themselves. We are challenged with change and most of us start to question the realness of the friendship or relationship. This is one of the moments when loyalty convicts us. Can you stand by the person you love or are friends with when they change? Will they stand by you when you change? So many people walk away from acquaintances when they feel they have "changed", but they never take the time to assess or explore that change. Do you have the strength to love someone when they change? The truth is this: we all will change and will continue to go through various changes as we grow and age. Some change we will love and embrace, some change we will hate, and some change will challenge us. However, we can't run away from the fact that the people we like, love, and relate to will change. We find balance in whether or not we will remain loyal to the people we are in relationship with because they will change. Remember loyalty is not just a word; it is a decision and a conviction that is held strongly in our actions to be committed and consistent.

When we love with balance, we should have a strong ability and desire to show affection to the ones we love. Our friends want to know they are loved by us. Our significant others, our partners or our spouses want to know that they are loved, not just by our words or our loyalty; they want to see it in our actions. They want to experience the fondness we have for them with all their senses or at least the senses that are within the appropriate boundaries of the relationship. Showing affection appears to have become very limited and confined to nice says or captions on social media. I know it isn't the case for every person, but showing affection seems to be trapped in quick texts or rapid post updates. There is nothing wrong with showing love and affection through social media, but it shouldn't be the only avenue in which you show love. I believe both men and women crave affection on all levels. Everyone wants to feel special; they want to hear that they are loved; they want to see that you thought about them in a very kind and thought out way.

Showing affection shouldn't be an option when you are loving with balance. A hug, a kiss, a nice note, flowers, a special date, attending a friend's special event, receiving a gift, planning a special outing, holding someone when they are down, building someone up with kind words, remembering a special day, celebrating with people, cuddling next to the fire, whispering

Love Me Right or Not At All

sweet words into their ear, comforting them during hard times, being a strong support for them, giving someone a helping hand, providing a listening ear, wiping away tears; these are just some of the ways that you can show affection to the people you love. Please don't get lost in the fantasy of showing affection.

What I mean is this: we sometimes feel that if we aren't extravagant or if we don't spend a whole lot of money it doesn't count for showing affection. To be honest with you, some people won't remember the horse carriage ride, the 24 orders of white roses, or the expensive jewelry; they will appreciate it possibly in that moment, but what they will always remember and forever cherish is that well placed kiss that they needed, or the hug that they thought about after a long hard day, or they will remember that, when they were putting themselves down and feeling sorry for themselves, you were right there listening to them, wiping away tears, and telling them how amazing they are. That type of affection and intimacy is scarce today. We are so busy or distracted, we have a false sense of connection through email, instant messenger, and video streaming that we have lost the art of being present in a room with the person we love. It is amazing how we can share a home with someone, share intimate space with someone, and make life plans with someone but you sit on opposite ends of the couch and barely say two words unless it is necessary. In most cases you know that you are disconnected, but neither person says anything to keep the peace within the home. We are functioning on autopilot, but because it is working or there is "peace", we will spend time in isolated unhappiness just to avoid issues.

    We are starving for affection, to be acknowledged and loved by our significant other, but we stay quiet because we fear rejection or being dismissed by the person we crave affection from. Communication is vital to healthy relationships and the conversation about needing and wanting affection has to be had. It won't happen just because you walk around sad or you're intentionally quiet, there is a conversation that has to happen so that your needs are expressed and the needs of your significant other can be expressed. It could be that a friend hasn't spoken to you in a while or hasn't invited you out to events; you have to let them know what you are feeling and then discuss with them a solution. It won't happen if you distance yourself; this stands the chance of making them more distant from you.

Showing affection and receiving affection are important in any relationship. For some it is as simple as holding hands or hugging, for others it could be holding each other before bed or watching a romantic movie snuggled up close. Affection is devotion towards another person or showing enthusiasm about someone. It is a wonderful feeling when someone shows you that they are passionate about being friends with you or excited about being in a relationship with you. I don't really know the reason why we lose that excitement about the ones we love, the ones who are loyal to us, and the ones who fight with us; I can tell you, though, that there will be a void when you don't show affection or you're not receiving affection. Loving with balance is more than just words, it is action. You can't just say, "But they know how much I love them!" You can't just say it; you have to show it too!

Giving space to someone is difficult. There isn't a gauge or instruction manual on when or how to give space. I can't even truly tell you when there is an appropriate time to give space to someone, but I do know that every human being needs space and time to themselves. Giving space is an important tool in having a successful and healthy relationship on all levels. Sometimes we are unable to think and process what we are feeling or reflect on life because we are consumed by our roles. For some, we have to be good friends, role models, and the model employee. For others, we have to be responsible bosses, providers, leaders, and parents. On top of all that responsibility, we often have to also be good husbands, wives, partners, spouses, significant others, boyfriends, or girlfriends. We have to manage our own emotions and dive deep into the management of the emotions of those we are intimately connected to.

Love Me Right or Not At All

When do you have space to just breathe? When do they have space to just think about what they want and need? This causes an imbalance in our relationships and, while we strive to maintain the people we love, we neglect the other person who needs to be healthy too—that's you. Remember a healthy relationship doesn't start with the other person; a healthy relationship starts with a healthy you. When you and another person decide to become friends, decide to date, decide to become intimate, or decide to become married, you both should have a healthy sense of self and a healthy sense of when you need space to just be alone and gather yourself. That is why the title of this chapter says you have to give space when needed. It should have been give or take space when needed, but to point back to the Starting Point: Love with Balance, we have to look at how we can make the decision to help those we love walk towards a healthy love for themselves and a healthy balance in the relationship. We give space when needed because they ask for space or we sense that space is needed. We recognize or we should be working to recognize when we are in need of space. Space isn't trying to "get away" from someone or taken because they "annoy us", it should be a moment to just escape from the pressures of daily roles and just reflect or center ourselves so that we can find clarity. We take space so that we can think and become a better us. We all need some room to hear ourselves think, to reflect on how we could have handled a situation better or a different way, and oftentimes we need the space to make sure that we are giving our best in every situation. Other times we need space to keep from saying or doing the wrong things; again, the purpose of asking for space or taking some space in a healthy relationship shouldn't be to avoid conflict, escape difficult situations, or to go out and "do you", taking space is just some time to be able to think clearly and freely.

There are some people who only need space once in a while; others need it on a consistent basis. However, I want to be clear that asking for space or allowing for space shouldn't be thought of in a negative way, shouldn't be used as an excuse to cheat, shouldn't be used as a punitive method towards those you love, and shouldn't be forced isolation. Taking some time for space should be done in a positive way and seen as a gateway to gaining balance and understanding. We may take the space to just clear our minds or we may take the space because we are feeling overwhelmed. Sometimes we take the space to just have uninterrupted time to do the things that we enjoy—like reading a book, writing in our journal, or binge-watching our favorite show. The space that we take may even be needed because we are deciding whether or not to remain in the relationship, but in this case we need to be sure that we have a serious and honest conversation with the person we are in a relationship with. We shouldn't take the space to avoid tough situations or difficult conversations. The space is given or taken because we just need some time to ourselves to think and unwind. Yes, there are times when you work things out and you unwind with your best friend or significant other, but there are times when you truly just need to be alone and that should be allowed.

Love Me Right or Not At All

We can't hold people hostage because we are afraid to allow them some space. We also can't be so consumed or selfish with them being in our presence that we don't allow them to be individuals. We give space to people because we recognize that even we need space. It doesn't mean we need to be away from the person forever, but we give them the freedom to take some time to themselves. Space can be a powerful tool for renewal and help people appreciate the time they do get to spend with the ones they love. Loving with balance means you love someone and allow them space when they need it. It also means you are able to ask for space as well.

STARTING POINT 4: LOVE WITH BALANCE

Be in Charge of Your Own Happiness

If you started at the beginning then we have been on quite a journey. We had to get over ourselves, let go of the masked version of ourselves, push the reset button, revive our dreams, manage love the right way with the right people, and now we are beginning to love with balance. Maybe you have decided to start right here because you want to take charge of your own happiness first and work your way to the first starting point. Whatever the reason, you are here and this chapter is focused on letting go of the assumption that your happiness is managed by others.

For so long we have placed the responsibility of our own happiness in the hands of other people. Some of these people were loving and caring; these individuals tried their best to make and keep us happy. We have placed our happiness into the hands of people who really didn't value us and they surely didn't care about our happiness. They only cared about what we could do for them or how happy we made them; yet we still placed our happiness into their hands. The truth is, whether they have good or bad intentions towards us, we should strive not to put such a heavy responsibility on someone else. We also should work really hard not to put happiness into materials, possessions, or our jobs; these are things that could change without notice. If we conclude that our happiness is governed by people or by things, we will find ourselves very unhappy in startling and rapid intervals. We place our happiness in ideas or potential; we place our happiness in people based on fictional adaptations of what we believe relationships and friendships are. When our stories or ideas of people and relationships don't have the "happy end to our lives" we were expecting we end up very disappointed and unhappy. When the people we are friends with, dating, or the people we marry don't live up to the potential that we see in them, we can become very pessimistic or cynical towards love, friendship, and marriage. This isn't the fault of the people we allowed control over our happiness; instead it is our fault and we have to be accountable and own up to the mistake we made.

Nothing or no one should be in charge of our happiness. It is an unrealistic expectation for someone to be the be all and end all of your happiness or the happy that is written in your story. As stated, people change, people evolve, people disconnect, people can be zombies and drain you, some people are often fickle or indecisive; some people are prone to depression, fear, anxiety, anger, rage, and even manipulation. We are also prone to these things, so why would we place our happiness in someone else or allow them to place their happiness in our hands? I know some people will read this and say, "I don't have people like that in my life," or "I would never do that to someone who placed their happiness in my hands." Unfortunately, we are so imperfect or fallible that even our best intentions will fall short. Why would you want to put that amount of pressure on someone or on yourself? They work hard

Love Me Right or Not At All

to keep you happy or you work very hard to keep them happy, but they are often sad, moody, unappreciative, frustrated, or can't even comprehend your efforts. How do you think they will feel when they see that even their best efforts to make you happy aren't working? How do you feel when you have been trying very hard to make someone happy and they tell you that you don't make them happy, or they tell you that they see you have been trying, but it isn't enough? How do you feel? What do you do?

This, I believe, is what happens all the time in friendships and relationships. We have given too much power to others to make us happy or they have given us way too much power to make them happy. It then turns out that no one is happy. Instead we have a bunch of people walking around with regrets and resentments, searching aimlessly for someone else to make them happy and causing more destruction and imbalance along the way.

Love Me Right or Not At All

It is my strong belief that we have to be in charge of our own happiness. We have to put things into perspective; taking a look at what makes us happy and what causes a decline in that happiness. We should look at our strengths and limitations, finding happiness in doing our best or giving our all, but also not becoming self-deprecating and defeated when we come face to face with our limitations or failure. We take charge of our environment and we adapt successfully to changes or we change the environment so that it adapts to the changes we have made within ourselves.

Taking charge of our happiness means that we set the bar for what affects our happiness and not the other way around. Our circumstances should not shape who we are or how we feel; instead who we are should shape our circumstances. So many times we get trapped in unhappiness and depression because we are afraid or we are too stubborn to take charge and change our circumstances. We say we are strong and we say we can overcome anything, but as soon as something doesn't go our way, we blame others because we are no longer happy. We wait for people to come and pull us out of the rut we are in. We wait for people to change their ways so we can be happy again. We hold on to this false sense of happiness because it takes the responsibility away from us and it places it in the hands of other people. We do this so we can blame them for our unhappy state.

I strongly believe that happiness is a decision that we make and so if we decide to be happy, we will be happy. Happiness has to come from within and you have to realize that the only person responsible for your happiness is you. The way we think will often directly affect how we feel and behave. If we place all the control of our happiness in people or things we make ourselves susceptible to the fickleness and instability that people and material possessions will bring. Being vulnerable to the inconsistency of people and possession will leave you with inconsistent levels of happiness. Instead you have to be aware of your own happiness and take charge in the way you define, process, and experience happiness for yourself.

Love Me Right or Not At All

Happiness is often defined as a good life and free from challenges and the stresses of life. If this is the expectation for happiness, I don't know how anyone can find it. I think, besides letting other people be in control of our happiness, we need healthy and reasonable expectations for what makes us happy. I can't define what happiness should look like for you, you must take self-control over that and define happiness for yourself. However, I do think that it is unrealistic to believe that people should define your happiness. I think that it is unrealistic to place your happiness in your possessions, but I also think that if you believe happiness can only be found in the absence of challenges and obstacles, you're going to be unhappy a lot. Even the people with the most friends or the most money find themselves unhappy sometimes. This is where we gain perspective on how to set clear and healthy expectations for our own happiness: we become aware of what makes us unhappy and we learn not to avoid it but how to overcome that unhappiness.

Love Me Right or Not At All

Taking control over our own happiness lies in acknowledging that we will have moments when we will be unhappy. We take that acknowledgement and figure out coping skills that will help us process the unhappy moments and move forward in a positive way. We recognize that there will be moments when we will be unhappy, but we don't wallow in them. We process and progress through those moments, but we don't get swallowed up in them. When we take charge of our own happiness, we don't find ourselves in a black hole when people leave, when people disappoint us; we don't find ourselves in a dark place when we lose a job, or we lose possessions, instead we recognize that those things happened, we grieve if we must, but ultimately we find happiness that is within us and we press forward. We have struggled so long with trying to be happy. We thought that if we surrounded ourselves with lots of friends, we met the right person, we got married, and if we pursued a career that would provide us with a lot of money we would be happy. Some of you who are reading this may have all those nice, wonderful things, but have a hard time figuring out why you are faced with unhappiness. It is going to require you taking back your own happiness and being in charge of what makes you happy.

You must develop coping mechanisms that will help you get through the tough times and even if you have to tell some people goodbye, your happiness won't go with them. It may be hard to believe, but a healthy you can choose whether to be happy or not. I'm not talking about individuals who may be dealing with some mental health challenges or even individuals who may have suffered loss or trauma, but I am speaking to those of us who are on the journey towards becoming healthy and having healthy relationships; there is a need to take back control of your own happiness.

You can take back control of your own happiness by redefining what makes you happy and what within you helps you make the choice to be happy regardless of your circumstances. It isn't that you need to ignore bad things when they happen or challenges when they come, it isn't healthy to be in denial or to be delusional, but it is making the choice to be happy because you understand that your happiness should come from within and not from other people or from the environment. Who we are truly has to shape our circumstances. If we let every bad situation, every failed relationship, or every failed friendship shape who we are we will never find happiness.

Taking control of your happiness means that you set the tone for your happiness, you set the expectations and they can change when you need them to, and you set the atmosphere when you come around. Again, this doesn't mean you do it in an arrogant way, but you do it in an assertive and confident way. You know those people who walk in the room and bring the sun and bring kindness with them. Being in charge of your happiness means that you have balance to your thinking and you understand the reality that not everyone will like you or embrace your happiness, but that doesn't stop you from being happy. The greatest indicator that you know you're in charge of your own happiness is that you don't try to diminish or drown out the happiness of others when you are at a low point. This is a clear sign that you have taken charge of your own happiness when you can celebrate others genuinely even when you're not feeling all that great. It is often said that "misery loves company" and I believe that people drag others down with them because they have spread out the control of their happiness among people and possessions.

    We have to revise the way we think about our own happiness and understand how sacred it is. When we conceptualize how precious our own happiness is, we won't be tempted to infringe upon the happiness of others. It isn't always going to be easy trying to maintain control of your own happiness because we have been taught that other people and many things will make us happy. We are taught that marriage or lifelong relationships will keep us happy, but the truth is those things alone won't make us happy. Our friends, family, significant others, our success, and our possessions should add to our happiness but not shape the

Love Me Right or Not At All

entirety of our happiness. Strive to take charge of your own happiness by focusing on what you want and what goals you want to achieve, and make the choice to be happy. When you have control of your own happiness you can love with balance. When you have control of your own happiness you can love others unselfishly. When you have control of your own happiness you can shape your circumstances and not let them shape who you are. Remember you're the only one who can truly make you happy, everyone else should just add to it.

STARTING POINT 5: ENJOY THE LOVE YOU'RE IN

The Here and Now Love

After all that work it is now time for you to enjoy your relationships—embracing the new you, taking off the mask of guilt and shame, loving the right people, and loving with balance. I can't quantify what reading this book or doing the work meant for you; however, the journey for me has been both invigorating and tumultuous. Writing this book wasn't just putting words to paper, it was an experience. I think that is why it took so long to write it. There aren't a lot of words or a lot of pages, the chapters aren't very long, but in each page and each starting point I lived it. I experienced it! It has taken some time for me to embrace the here and now and finally enjoy my relationships because change is hard. If you have changed your focus from your past, it is time to focus on what is happening now. We have often found ourselves stuck in the past and stuck in past hurt and we miss out on the goodness and the love that is right in front of us. I think it would be a waste if you did all the hard work of becoming a healthy you and you don't enjoy the love that is taking place in the here and now.

Put your focus on the love you have right now, not on the love you used to have, and not on the love you think you will have in the future. If you are focused on what is happening right now you can see what the people who love you are bringing to the table, you can hear what they are seeing, and you can embrace what they appreciate about you. When we look back at past relationships or even what your current relationship used to be, we diminish the work and the change that the person we are relating to has done and we completely ignore the change that has happened within us. We can focus on who we are now and what is great about who we are now. When we have that awareness, we can share with our friends and significant other what makes us happy, what our strengths are, and what we appreciate about the relationships. We can focus on what they do for us and how they love us, and show them affection based on understanding that everyone needs affection rather than just showing affection when they show us affection. When we love in the here and now we can pay attention to the people who are in our lives at the present time and we can assess what their attentions are towards us and our relationships. This assessment will also keep us sharp and help us avoid inviting unwanted people into the love we are trying to enjoy. Unwanted people are either going to distract you from being with the ones who love you or they are going to try to deter you from enjoying the love you're in because they are unhappy or miserable.

Let me just say that not everyone is out to get you! I don't want you to just spend time giving people "eviction notices", but if you are focused on the here and now I believe you can see clearly who is around you and you'll give out invitations to the right people to share in the love you're trying to enjoy. When you can enjoy the love you're in and have a clear perspective of who you invite into your love you'll be able to truly have fun! I think that is what we miss out on; in trying to be perfect, trying to cross out everything on our "lists", and trying to be the best we miss out on having fun. Hang out with your friends, spend quality time with family, and date your spouse, partner, or significant other like you did when you first got together. We don't take enough time to have fun anymore. We are so caught up in our routines, our jobs, and the long-term goals that we forget to just have fun and enjoy one another. It then leads us to be sad, bored, and resentful because we don't have any fun. I'm not saying that being responsible and taking care of business isn't important, but we still need to include fun in our relationships as well. Laughter is truly good medicine and enjoying the company of those you love will help you strengthen the relationships that you have. So take time in the here and now to enjoy the love you're in and remember to have as much fun as you can.

EVALUATE IT ALL

We are embracing the new, free, and unmasked versions of ourselves. We are living in our truth or we are working towards living in the truth of who we truly are. We are beginning to heal from the exposure of the truth and we are acknowledging the process of healing. We are starting to set realistic expectations for ourselves and those we love. We recognize that no one owes us anything and that we have to love ourselves first so we can effectively love others. That is what this final chapter is all about, evaluating everything that we have learned, read, and processed. I want you to understand that relationships don't go in a straight line and neither does this book. Just like our lives and our relationships, things kind of go in a cycle. So we may have several moments of going back over the chapters, revisiting the starting points, and changing our perspectives; I want you to know that it is OK! Whatever you have to do to be healthy and have healthy relationships I want you to do it. Don't be afraid to

Love Me Right or Not At All

take off the mask and if it comes back take it off again. Remember not to pick at the scabs when the healing begins and also remember that it is OK to hit the reset button, restart, renew, and refresh your thinking, your feelings, and even your relationships. There is nothing wrong with a reset or a fresh start.

Evaluation is a powerful tool and it helps us to identify our strengths and our limitations. Evaluation pushes us to check out what worked and what didn't. It encourages us not to get comfortable in our relationships or to become complacent in the maturing that has to occur as we grow and age in life. Sometimes dead people and dead places will creep back into our lives, but, if we are reviewing the lessons we have learned and we are evaluating the goals we have set, we can remove those people from our lives. Don't forget that there is no life in graveyards and zombies only crave to eat living organisms to make them dead like them. We may have to ask some people to leave and grant them permission to leave as well.

Love Me Right or Not At All

Evaluate, review, assess, revamp, revise, and revisit whatever starting point or principle you need to in order to reach your healthy self. At the beginning or end of this book I want you to achieve not just your best self, but the healthiest version of yourself. I want the healthy you to love yourself and others the right way. I want you to be confident when you tell yourself, "I must love me the right way!" I want you to be assertive when you tell others, "Love me right or not at all!" I believe that we can become healthy and have healthy relationships.

Made in the USA
Middletown, DE
16 April 2016